BECOMING

—— an ——

AMERICAN FAMILY

Ned M Cole, Jr.
Edited by Mary Carol Cole

INKS & BINDINGS

Inks and Bindings
888-290-5218
www.inksandbindings.com
orders@inksandbindings.com

CONTENTS

DEDICATION

This book is dedicated to my deceased son Jonathan Ned Cole.

This story about the life and times of Ned M Cole, Jr's family is for my children and my grandchildren so that they and future generations of Cole's will know their history. A special thanks to my grandson Jeffry A. Reilly, who encouraged me to tell this story so that one day he could tell it to his grandchildren.

Perhaps one day my grandchildren will enjoy telling their children and grandchildren about the long history of their American family. Perhaps each of them and the generations of Cole descendants to come will in their own way contribute to making America a little bit better place. And just maybe by telling this story for them, they will not forget those Americans who came before them.

ACKNOWLEDGEMENTS

A special thanks to my wife Carol whose tireless efforts to study the genealogy of her family and to document the births, deaths and many facts included in this book. And, a very special thanks to her for editing and correcting many of the details I have written.

An equally special thanks to Craig Coberly, (my brother-in-law) Jean Boggio (my cousin and an author of a book called STOLEN FIELDS) and Steve Maxi (my several times removed cousin) for the countless hours they spent researching the history of the Cole family and generously sharing their research with Carol and me.

Nearly all of the geology facts included in this book are from the research material provided by these intrepid researchers.

A heartfelt thanks to all of you.

PREFACE

More than likely this story would not have found its way to paper had it not been for the encouragement of my grandson, Jeffrey Reilly. Over the years I have related many of the stories my father told me to Jeff. A few months ago, he told me that he could not remember all the details of what I related to him. He told me that one day he would like to tell the stories to his grandchildren while they sat on his knee.

Many of the details of this story could not have been told without the many stories told to me by my father, Ned M. Cole. My dad was quite a story teller. He related to me many incidents in his life and all he could remember about his mother, Helen (Henderson) Cole and his father, Everson Porter Cole.

When I was a small boy, my grandfather Everson P Cole and I slept in the same bed. He many times told me stories about his life. Some of them I remembered. What I remember I included in this story.

This story begins with the family origins in Great Britain, Ireland and Lichtenstein. It continues with the families immigration from Wales and Lichtenstein, their trials and triumphs from the Revolutionary War, the Civil War, both World Wars, Korean War, the Vietnam War and Afghanistan. The story tells about the deaths of some of the current generation and the personal stories of Coles yet living. The treads of all these stories come together to form the fabric of America.

CHAPTER 1

The Early Coles' Story

The Cole surname most likely originated about one thousand years ago in the British Isles at the time of the Norman conquest of the British Islands. Old English references to the word "col," meaning coal for swarthy, may also explain the origin of the name. One very early family motto was *Deum cole, regem serva*, meaning "Worship God, and serve the King."

My direct line of ancestors and their wives' ancestors have a long martial history. Thirteen served during the Revolutionary War and seven served in the Civil War. At least five of my related relatives served in World War II. Early records establish that the Henderson family, from whom my grandmother Helen Elizabeth (Henderson) Cole, is descended, fought and died in Scotland in 1450 serving the Scottish king. The Coles' and their wives' ancestors have fought in nearly if not all wars in which Americans have fought and died. Although I did not fight in any American wars, I like to think that, given my twenty-seven years during which I served in the United States Air Force, I continued my family tradition of serving our nation. My son, Jeffrey James Cole, continued the tradition by serving in the Illinois National Guard. And my grandson, Jeffrey Reilly, became a United States Marine Corps officer. My direct ancestor, Willam Carrol fought at the Cowpens during the Revolutionary War. He was born in Pennsylvania in 1741 and died in Mercer County, Pennsylvania in 1813. He was detached with the Cumberland County Militia on October 23, 1777 as a sub-lieutenant under Captain Askey. At the time of the Cowpens battle he was a captain. Joseph Carrol also fought at Cowpens.

In the early 1600s, the Coles immigrated to America from Northern Ireland and settled around Wells, Maine. Where they emigrated from in Northern Ireland is not known. At the time that the Coles immigrated, Maine was a part of Massachusetts. Maine ultimately became a state on March 20, 1820. Where exactly in the British Isles from which the Coles emigrated is not known. Other sources suggest that they came from Wales. However, Wales may not be correct. Possibly, Wales may have been confused with Wells, Maine.

This chronicle of the Cole family would not at all be complete without telling the tale of Goody (real name Eunice) Cole and her husband, William Cole of Hampton, New Hampshire. In 1656, Eunice (Goody) was accused, tried, and convicted, along with her husband, of being a witch. They were both sentenced to life in prison. Goody was locked up in a cave where she stayed until her death. After being incarcerated for several years, Goody petitioned in 1672 for release. But lacking any funds to pay arrears or pay bail, she was unable to secure her release. To ward of any future mischief by wooden stake was driven her heart. Goody is mentioned in a poem by John G. Whittier, her husband died in 1662 at the age of eighty-one. Upon Goody's death, she was buried in an unmarked grave, WRECK AT REVESMEUTH.

My father claimed that there were horse thieves and Native Americans in the Cole background, but never offered any proof. His mother, Helen Cole, steadfastly denied there was any truth to Dad's tales. My dad enjoyed making up tales to amuse us children. It would seem that Dad passed the gene on to me.

On my grandmother (Henderson) Cole's side, her ancestors emigrated from Scotland.

I am directly descended from Samuel Cole, his son John Cole, his son James Gowen Cole, his son George Washington Cole, his son Augustus Porter Cole, his son Everson Porter Cole, and his son Ned McCaughtry Cole. My son is Jeffrey James Cole, the last male Cole in my direct line. My son has no children.

John Cole's grandson, Augustus P. Cole, my great-grandfather, married Mary Ann Dickson (born on Neville Island, Pennsylvania), whose Dickson family emigrated from Wigtownshire, Scotland, to Prince Edward Island, Canada, in 1822 and from there to Plattsburg, New York. Mary Ann married Augustus P. Cole in 1870 at Manchester Hill, Allegheny County, Pennsylvania.

Mary Ann was the daughter of James Dickson, my great-great-grandfather. James Dickson was born on April 30, 1832, on Prince Edward Island, Canada. From Plattsburg, the Dickson family moved to Pittsburgh, Pennsylvania, and from there to Neville Island, Pennsylvania.

The earliest American ancestor I was able to find was Samuel Cole, a resident of Boston.

He immigrated to America on the *Winthrop Fleet* in 1630. Samuel owned an inn in Boston called the Three Mariners. Henry Wadsworth Longfellow wrote a play mentioning the inn and a character in the play named Samuel Cole. Samuel was born in 1597 somewhere in the British Isles. He was a member of the Honorable Artillery Company, the first military organization in America.

My great-great-great-grandfather, John Cole, son of Samuel Cole, an early settler of Wells, Maine, was commissioned as captain in the Continental Army by John Hancock. Captain Cole served in the Continental Army, Fourth Company, First Regiment commanded by Colonel Noah Moulton. Some records suggest that he may have advanced to the rank of major. DAR records state that John Cole was awarded four thousand dollars, most likely for equipping his own unit. According to *Revolutionary War Bounty Land Grants Awarded by States*, John was born April 19, 1740, in Wells, York

County, Maine District, Massachusetts, where he married his first wife (my great-great-great-grandmother), Abigail Gowen. Originally, Massachusetts did not have a land grant program. Many states were very generous, giving to veterans up to one thousand five hundred acres. Eventually, Massachusetts did institute a program. In John Cole's case, his surviving wife, Polly, was granted two hundred acres in 1835.

According to research done by a DAR friend, Elizabeth Gill, John Cole married Susanna Hutchinson, who had escaped the massacre of her family by New York State Indians. Carol and I have not been able to confirm this lineage by her own research. The John Cole named in Gill's research may not be the same Cole from whom I am descended.

James Gowen Cole, John Cole's son, my great-great-grandfather, was born in Wells, Maine, on August 25, 1773. He died in Allegheny town in 1810.

One of my early relatives, Arthur Bragdon (second wife, Mary), was born in 1597 in Stratford-upon-Avon, home of William Shakespeare. Arthur was nineteen years old when William Shakespeare died, so most likely he knew Shakespeare. Arthur's family earned their living as butchers. I wonder if Shakespeare ate some of their meat. Arthur immigrated to York, Maine, aboard sailing ship, *Hopewell,* or possibly another of the Winthrop fleet about 1636.

In 1820 Maine became a state. My great-great-grandfather, George Washington Cole, whose father was James Gowen Cole, along with his brothers, James, William, Ivory, and Rufus, migrated in covered wagons from Maine to Neville Island. George was the son of John Cole, my great-great-great-great-great- grandfather, a Revolutionary War veteran. The brothers purchased three hundred acres, which encompassed most of the north end of the island. The land was originally awarded to Captain Neville for his contributions to the nation during our Revolutionary War. All the land was heavily forested. The brothers cut down the trees and sold the wood to Ohio

River steamboats. The alluvial soil on the island from centuries of flooding was very fertile. After they cleared the land, they began to farm. Soon, their produce began to appear on the streets of Pittsburgh. George W. Cole was born in Maine in 1798 and died on Neville Island on December 28, 1875. As the family prospered, their farm grew, and they began to can vegetables for sale in Pittsburgh. One of their biggest customers for their produce and a competitor for their canned goods was what became the H. J. Heinz Company. A few other New Englanders migrated to Neville Island, cleared their land, and began to truck farm their plots. I am related to some of the Coles' neighbor farmers, the Braddons, the Hamiltons, and Dicksons. The island became one of the primary sources of food for the growing city of Pittsburgh. The population of Neville Island was 236 in 1860. The population of Pittsburgh around the start of the Civil War was 49,221. Neville Island was incorporated as a township on April 8, 1854. Churches, schools, houses, and merchant shops sprung up around the Island. A town center began to form. All the farmer families on the island knew each other and regularly mingled together. A few young ladies married their neighbors' sons. By the start of the Civil War, Neville Island was a thriving and prosperous community. Life was good. Little did they know then that e vents would descend upon them early in the twentieth century, which would forever change the lives of those who lived, worked, loved, died, and prospered on their thriving island.

George and Dorcus (Bragdon) Cole had five children: Augustus, Carrie, George, Henrietta, and Milton.

George Washington Cole's son, Augustus Porter Cole, my great grandfather, took over the farm upon his father's death and continued to build the enterprise. Augustus P. Cole was born in Allegheny City on May 2, 1836, and died on the Neville Island in 1901. In the mid- or late 1800s, Augustus was educated at Mount Union College, Ohio. College-educated folks were quite rare at the time, but the Cole family believed in education. E. P. Cole, my grandfather, was wealthy enough to educate his two oldest daughters, Gladys and Coreen, beyond high school. Both earned bachelor's degrees.

Ivory Cole, brother of George Washington Cole, along with James Cole Junior, George Cole, and others formed a company to build a bridge across the Ohio River at the southern end of Neville Island. Pennsylvania Act No. 625 passed on March 24, 1860, authorized the forming of the company. George Cole donated part of his land for the bridge. A wooden-structure bridge named Fleming Park Bridge was built in the early 1860s. In 1894, it was replaced by a metal structure. Today, a steel structure stands in its place.

The picture of Augustus included in the end section of this book is a black and white charcoal portrait that Augustus commissioned when he was about thirty-five or forty years old. My dad handed the portrait down to me. On a move from Denville, New Jersey, with my family, my children (all five of whom were living with my wife and me at the time) jumped in to help with the packing. They knew how important the painting of Augustus was to me. They took it out of its frame and rolled it up in a rug. The painting never made it to our new home in Murrysville, Pennsylvania. Fortunately, we had taken a picture of the painting and were able to commission an artist to recreate the painting. It hangs today in my home in Melbourne, Florida.

Augustus Cole enlisted in 1862 in Company K, 123rd Pennsylvania Volunteer Infantry commanded by Colonel Clark and was assigned to Fifth Corp, Army of the Potomac. Augustus fought at Fredericksburg, Antietam, South Mountain, and Chancellorsville. At one of the battles, probably Chancellorsville, he was wounded. Family oral history has it that Augustus wrote a letter home in which he informed his family that he was wounded, but not to worry. He told them that he was not going to tell them where he was wounded because they would know which direction he was going when he was shot. He was honorably discharged from the army when his enlistment was up.

After recovering from his wound, Augustus returned to Neville Island to resume his life as a farmer. Apparently, Augustus had enough of war. He was one of the original ninety-day enlistees, so with his enlistment up and his wound behind him, he was not obligated to reenlist. One does not have to guess that his family convinced him with not much effort that he had done his part. In any event he did not reenlist. I know little more about my great- grandfather's participation in the Civil War. Perhaps some more research will reveal more details. History books reveal that Augustus belonged to the Republican Party as do I.

My great-grandfather on my grandmother Helen Elisabeth (Henderson) Cole's side, her father, Harvey Heath Henderson, enlisted as a private in Company G, 39 Regiment PA, Tenth Reserve Infantry, Union Army at Mercer on July 8, 1861. His unit saw action at Bull Run, Antietam, Fredericksburg, South Mountain, the Wilderness, Mine Run, Gettysburg, Spotsylvania, Spotsylvania Court House, and a few other engagements. His unit had 207 men. Many more were wounded. Harvey was soon promoted to musician. At the time, musicians served as musicians and battle signalmen, but also had the job of tending to the dead and wounded. My family's oral history has it that Harvey was one of those hunkered down behind a stone wall at Fredericksburg covered by bodies six deep. After the war, Harvey moved to North Dakota, where he became a successful cobbler. He died in Taylor, North Dakota. Harvey regularly returned to Pennsylvania to visit his wife and several children. Many times, Harvey asked his family to move to Dakota. My great- grandmother, Lucretia Henderson, refused. Nevertheless, Harvey stayed in touch with his family and regularly sent them support money. Sadly, my great-grandmother told only a tale of their father abandoning his family. Through my dad's generation and mine, Harvey was pictured as a deadbeat father. Luckily, my father and I visited Harvey's grandson and was told the rest of the story. Harvey most likely suffered from extreme PTSD because of the thousands he witnessed being killed and horribly wounded. I know for certain that Harvey fought at Gettysburg. I touched his name carved on a monument. Harry Henderson married Lucretia Kirk Henderson. She was born in Niles, Ohio. Lucretia was the daughter of Thomas B. Kirk.

After the Battle of Gettysburg, Harvey's brother was sent to Gettysburg from Washington, DC to aid in the recovery and burial of thousands of Gettysburg dead.

Harvey's widow, Lucretia Henderson, petitioned in 1891 for a pension due to Harvey's service in the Civil War.

Harvey Henderson's parents were Jonathan Henderson and Elizabeth Brown. Elizabeth Brown's father was Clark Rathbone. Clark Rathbone was born on 1760 in Exeter, Washington, Rhode Island. Clark served in 1778 in Captain Joseph Draper's Company, a subordinate unit of General John Sullivan.

Jonathan Henderson's Revolutionary War parents were Mary Carroll and John Carnahan Henderson. Mary was the daughter of William Carroll. William fought in the Battle of Cowpens. Captain Carroll forced at sword point his men that were exhausted to continue marching. Four of his men who were very weary slipped off to sleep in a barn. The British burned the barn and only one escaped alive. William served first as a private with the Cumberland County Militia (Pennsylvania). Later, he served as an officer under Captain Askey. In Captain Askey's unit, William was promoted to captain.

On another side tale, Ebenezer Bragdon, to whom I am directly related, enlisted in Captain Sullivan's Company during the Revolutionary War on or about July 28, 1779. He was born about 1745 in Maine and died on May 25, 1807, in Sullivan, Hancock County, Maine.

In the meantime, Augustus Cole continued to improve his truck garden land and modernize his ketchup and other produce canning plant. Business was booming. One of their primary crops was asparagus. I remember an asparagus field located on my grandfather Everson P. Cole's Sandy Lake, Pennsylvania, farm on what seemed to me, as a little boy, very long rows of asparagus. Many times as a child, we enjoyed eating asparagus deliciously prepared by my grandmother, Helen (Henderson) Cole, at many dinners that we enjoyed at the Sandy Lake House where the Cole family moved after losing their Neville Island home to the United States Government.

The family moved from Neville Island to Sandy Lake about 1919. Shortly after eviction from Neville Island was certain, my grandfather, E. P. Cole, contracted to buy some land in Virginia. The land deal turned out to be a fraud. My grandfather's fortune started to dwindle away. But my grandfather continued to try to win back the fortune the United States government had taken from him. In the 1920s, he invested most of what cash he had left in the stock market. In 1929, Grandpa lost over a hundred thousand dollars. He kept trying but was never able to make a comeback. One of his last acts in his late eighties was to give to me one of his inventions in the hopes that I would be able to make something of it. The invention was a good one for earlier years, but technology had passed his invention by. I was not able to make the invention a commercial success. Grandpa died with little more than the clothes on his back.

On Augustus's land not far from the banks of the Ohio River, he, or perhaps his father, built what at the time was a large white clapboard house. A picture of that house survives to this day. Augustus married Mary Ann (Hamilton) (Dickson) Cole in 1812. Mary Ann Hamilton's parents were born in Pennsylvania. Mary Ann's grandparents were born in Northern Ireland. In the 1800s, Augustus and his wife, Mary Ann, had two children, and one of whom was my grandfather, Everson Porter Cole. Everson had only one brother, James A. Cole. Everson, known to most as E. P. Cole, was born on October 10, 1887, on Neville Island. Everson Cole died on September 11, 1966, near Syracuse, New York. He was survived by his wife, Helen Cole, and children, Ned M. Cole Sr., Robert Cole, Coreen (Cole), Frith, and Gladys (Cole) Burnhoft. Everson's mother, Mary Ann (Dickson) Cole, long survived her husband. She was born on August 18, 1845, the oldest of ten children. She did not die until April 27, 1933, at the age of eighty-eight.

According to family legend, Mary Ann Cole was a tough old girl not to be trifled with by her children nor her neighbor farmers, who lived on the island, nor the United States government, who eventually ran her off her land.

In 1985, my cousin Marion Bernhoft, daughter of Gladys (Cole) Bernhoft, interviewed my father and he related to Marion all that he could remember about his family home and his grandmother, Mary Ann. The full text of that interview may be found in Appendix B.

My father left the island when he was six years old. Nevertheless, he retained quite vivid memories about his life on Neville Island.

Marion asked him: "Do you remember your grandmother (Mary Ann) and the home you lived in?" My father recalled that his grandmother, Mary Ann, was a rather stately woman and always liked to wear expensive clothes. She lived in one part of the house. Dad's mother, father, sisters, and brother lived in the other half. He remembered going into a divided part of the house where his grandmother lived to eat breakfast. Every afternoon, my dad told Marion that he fetched a brown egg from their henhouse and would take it to Grandma. Every morning, she would have the brown egg for breakfast.

My dad remembered that his grandmother was tall, held herself very straight, but not necessarily beautiful. My dad was never ashamed to walk down the street with her dressed in her fine clothing and straight posture.

The Coles did not have an indoor bathtub or toilet in those days. Great Grandma Mary and all the children took a bath in a tub once a week.

Dad related that the house the family lived in was a substantial home and furnished very well. The home sat on a beautiful site a few yards from the Ohio River, from which he and his family enjoyed watching boats going up and down the river.

On the inside of the house was an especially beautiful cherry stairway, which grandly wound down to a landing. All the stairways in the house were carpeted.

According to my dad, he remembers his family as being quite well-off, if not rich. Dad did not recall any other families living on the island as being better off.

Outside the house in well-tilled fields, Dad recalled acres of produce, their many horses, mules, wagons, farm equipment, a large barn, and a pickle and horseradish factory. He vividly remembers the night someone burned down their pickle factory, which stood very close to their house. The night was a terrible night for my dad.

Dad recalled that soon the government came in with steam shovels and took the front steps right off their house. My dad remembered until his death one very frightening day when two men in uniforms came up to their house on horses and advised the family that they were required to vacate the house. Dad stood behind his mother clutching her dress. His father, wearing a six shooter, stood defiantly in the doorway facing the intruders. Burned into my dad's mind were his father's exact words: "The first man up, the first man down."

Eventually, the situation became dangerous for the family. My grandfather, Everson Cole, sent his wife and children to Sandy Lake, Pennsylvania, for their safety. Mary Ann refused to leave and stayed with my grandfather until the bitter end.

CHAPTER 2

Grandpa EP and Grandma Helen Elisabeth (Henderson) Cole's story

My grandfather, Everson Porter Cole, was born on Neville Island on October 10, 1877. Around late 1890s or early 1900s, Augustus told his son, Everson Porter Cole, known to friends and family as E. P., "Son, I have a proposition for you. We have many merchants in and around Pittsburgh who have not paid us for the produce and canned goods we delivered. You can keep whatever you can collect." He gave E. P. a list of the Pittsburgh merchants who were in arrears. At the time it was common for wealthy families to send their sons to Europe. E. P. set off onto the streets of Pittsburgh to pressure the merchants into paying up. Whether he used charm, guile, or threats, he collected a sizable sum. With a pocket full of cash, E. P. boarded a New York Central train out of Pittsburgh's central train station and headed for New York City. E. P. was about twenty years old at the time. As the train chugged along toward New York City, the excitement in E. P. began to build. After E. P. spent a few days touring the sites of the great city of New York, he booked passage on a steamship to London, England. Family tales did not record if Everson booked passage on a tramp steamer or luxury liner. Most likely, the voyage across the Atlantic was not filled with Titanic excitement and certainly not the drama. After more than a week sailing the ocean blues, Everson arrived in merry old England. Perhaps he spent some time traveling about the British Isles. Perhaps he spent some time looking for his ancestral homeland, which was thought to be Wales. Off then he went to the Continent. Paris, Amsterdam, Berlin, Vienna, and Rome may all have been destination points of his odyssey. My father remembered his father telling him about some time he spent in Spain. One wonders of the excitement he felt, the girls he met, the good times, scary times, and all the other possible adventures he encountered on his trek around Europe. What an exciting time it must have been for him. But those details we may never know. Many years later when I had the opportunity to ask my grandfather about his trip to Europe, I never thought to ask. I suspect at the time; I was unaware of him having made the trip. Close to a century later, his great-grandson, Jeffrey Reilly, embarked on a much similar European safari.

About to run out of funds, E. P. set sail for New York. A week or so later, he arrived back in New York City, broke, hungry, and ready to go home. He wired his father collect to wire enough for a train ticket to Pittsburgh. E. P.'s father probably verbally chastised his son but wired him enough to get home. No doubt Augustus grinned to himself, but never let on to his son. The prodigal son had returned. Under his father's tutelage, Everson learned the craft of farming and running a business. All the work on the farm was done by horse, mule, and by hand. The Coles employed four full-time workers and temporary ones during the height of the growing season. Exactly how many workers they employed at the peak of their enterprise is not known. What is known is that in 1918, all they had built over a century came crashing down.

After Augustus's death in 1901, his oldest son, my grandfather, Everson Porter Cole, took over management of the Cole truck farm and canning plant. Like his father, he continued to expand the business. Everson married my quite pretty grandmother, Helen Elisabeth (Henderson) Cole, on June 2, 1901.

Helen was born on June 27, 1879, in Sandy Lake, Pennsylvania. She died in 1975 in the same town at the age of ninety-seven.

Helen was a descendant of Robert Henderson of Hendersonville, Pennsylvania. According to my father, Helen Cole's heart was never on the island. Up to her death, her heart remained in her Hendersonville, Pennsylvania, birthplace. Nevertheless, being the dutiful wife that she was, she worked hard to help her husband while they lived on Neville Island.

By the early 1900s, the Cole family was known as one of the wealthiest families on the island. Everson was gearing up his canning operation to take on his main canning competitor, H. J. Heinz Company. The Cole enterprise had a significant advantage. In addition to having a canning plant, they had the land on which they could grow canning produce, feedstock, and direct access to the produce of other farmers on Neville Island. Then came World War I and the heavy hand of the United States government.

Around the turn of the century in 1900 (I am not sure of the time line of Grandpa Cole's story; I do not know if it was before or after E. P. married Helen, but I think after), my grandfather acquired a 1901 model Colt 38 special. This was around the time of Poncho Villa, so it must have been in the 1920s. He and a friend embarked on a copper prospecting trip to Mexico, packing their prospecting tools, camping equipment, grub, and their weapons. One sunny day, my grandpa was sitting on a slope by himself. His friend was off looking for prospecting sites. My grandpa jumped with a start when he heard the crack of a weapon nearby and felt the thud of a bullet hitting the ground close by his side. His first thought was they had been attacked by Poncho and his bandits. To his relief, it was his friend who had crept up close and shot a rattlesnake, which was crawling toward my grandpa. He and his friend packed up and fled Mexico. They never found any copper. The Colt 38 has a story of its own as it winds its way down through my family.

Grandpa had a continuing interest in mining. For a few months in the 1920s, he and some friends traveled to Colorado in search of mining opportunities. Apparently, they met with little success.

In 1918, the United States government decided that they needed a sizable chunk of Neville Island to build a munitions plant. The island, the government reasoned, was an ideally safe place to build a dangerous munitions plant. Through eminent domain, the government seized much of Neville Island farmland. My grandfather and his mother fought the government to the bitter end. This is one of the weapons my grandfather used to hold off U.S. Government agents for a time as they worked to take his land.

To shield his wife and children from the dangers that circled about all the farmers on the island, my grandfather shipped his family off to safer places. His oldest son, Robert Cole, stayed on with his father for a while. My father, Ned M Cole, was six years old when his father sent to safer ground near Hendersonville, Pennsylvania.

My father told me that he clearly remembered the trauma felt by his family and many details of his Neville Island home. Unfortunately, I no longer remember many of the details. Luckily, though, my older cousin, Marion (Cole) Bernhoft, interviewed my father in 1985 and recorded what my father told her.

One night during this period, someone set fire to my grandfather's factory. It was burned to the ground. My grandfather never learned who had set fire, but he always suspected that there was a connection to the United States government.

My father recalled that he remembered that after the blue-uniformed police rode away on their horses after informing his father that the family must vacate their home, Everson secured a metal tub in which he shot a neat circle of bullet holes in the bottom of the tub. Everson then placed the bullet-riddled tub along with six spent cartridges about fifty yards down the lane leading up to their home. Everson and his mother, Mary Ann, sat on the front porch of their house with pistols and shotgun in hand, and dared the government enforcers to step beyond the not-so-subtle hint suggested by the circle of bullet holes. According to a December 21, 1921, *New York Times* article, my grandfather was known to be a deadly shot with either his left or right hand. The police could clearly see my grandfather sitting on his front porch from morning until late at night with two revolvers, one in each hand, while his mother threatened with a shotgun across her lap. One of the revolvers that my grandfather possessed was most likely the 38-caliber Colt handed down to my father, then on to me, and then on to my grandson, Jeffrey Reilly. According to a 1919 *New York Times* article, my grandfather advised the police, "I am paying my bill in lead." When World War I ended and the government abandoned their plans to build a munitions plant, my grandfather and great-grandmother tried to recover their land. My grandfather complained that the government had offered only one-third of what the land was worth and even offered to lend the land to the government until the government no longer needed it. The government refused. My grandfather traveled by train to Washington DC to plead his case with the government to no avail. The Government put up for public auction all the land seized from the Nevelle Island farmers.

My grandfather was not able to outbid US Steel. While my grandfather was at the auction, he left his mother to guard their home. He told a *Times* reporter that his mother was just as good a shot as he was with "my two irons."

All the farmers whose land was confiscated had to leave the island. The deck was stacked against them by the government, US Steel, and others who wanted their land. It seems that the elite powers close to government bureaucrats had more pull than the Neville Island's dirt farmers. All the farmers asked for was that the government sell back to them the seized land for what the government paid. The government froze the farmers out. My grandfather and his mother were the last to leave the island. My grandfather refused to accept eviction papers from mounted police who came to the back door of their house to serve the eviction papers. When the police handed the papers out to my grandfather, my grandfather said, "I am not taking that, and I will give you this." He pulled out his two guns. The police chief (Lawrence) and his lieutenants left. Lawrence never returned.

Left with no choice, Everson and his mother left Neville Island to join his family, which he had temporarily housed near Hendersonville, Pennsylvania. Never one to give up in total defeat, Everson entered into a contract to buy a parcel of land in Virginia where he could continue his life as a farmer. The deal turned out be a land swindle.

With still enough funds from the government settlement, Everson purchased farming land outside the small town of Sandy Lake, Pennsylvania. The land had a house, a barn, and a few pieces of farming equipment. This original farmhouse had carbide lighting, but no electricity and no indoor plumbing. A small outhouse served the original owners for years. The old outhouse still stood when I visited the farm as a child.

According to my father, Everson took one look at the house and announced, "Tear it down. Just save the kitchen." On the same site, he built a new two-story house. The house for that time was quite modern. He had installed running water, bathtubs and sinks, and electric lighting throughout. My father related that the neighbors around the area saw the house and said, "Boy, that guy must be rich.

My father knew his family was not really rich, but certainly lived better than most families surrounding their farm. Soon, Everson bought a new car and truck, which impressed his neighbors even more. When telephones became available, Grandpa had one installed.

As a small child, I remember the old wood box, hand cranked-type phone hanging on the wall in Grandma's kitchen. The old box phone continued to function into the 1950s. I remember seeing it hanging on the wall.

According to my father, the farm supported seven acres of asparagus, many heads of cabbage, and twelve to twenty acres of potatoes. I remember the farm also having a large grove of golden, delicious, and red McIntosh apple trees. Many a time, Grandpa treated us small children with delicious-tasting apples. Originally, all farming was done by the help of horses and a great deal of hand labor. In 1922 or 1923, Grandpa bought a Studebaker truck. In 1924, Grandpa bought a Republic truck. Early on in Grandpa's farming activities in Sandy Lake, he built a large chicken house, which housed up to one thousand chickens. Grandpa and his workers candled every single egg and stamped them with a date. Consequently, he secured top prices from McCanns wholesaler. Grandpa's bad luck continued for after a couple of years of very profitable egg production, his chicken shed burned to the ground.

Undaunted by his string of bad luck, Grandpa decided to take the remaining funds he had and become a full-time stock trader. He set himself up in Pittsburgh, where he grew his funds into a sizable fortune. He told my father that he saw the 1929 crash coming but decided to "take one more turn." Grandpa took one turn too many. When the crash came, he lost most of his fortune. For a time, his family feared that because Everson was so despondent, he might commit suicide as many did at the time. Eventually he came out of his funk and was continue all throughout the Great Depression to provide well for his family.

Long after the time for a less optimistic man to give up, he kept trying. I remember visiting him in New York where he spent his last days living in my aunt Gladys's house; he gave me his last invention. It was a rope ladder he thought could save lives in the event of a hotel fire. As he gave his invention to me. He told me that he hoped I could do something with his invention. Sorry Grandpa. Time had passed his invention by.

The Sandy Lake house was situated about five miles north of the small town of Sandy Lake, Pennsylvania. The farmland and a house upon the land was about a mile north off the main highway to Sandy Lake. The house was situated on the corner of what I remember as the "State Gravel Road" and a dirt road leading the "back way," as it was called, to Sandy Lake. In the 1920s, both the main highway to Sandy Lake and the State Gravel Road were most likely dirt. I clearly remember playing in the front yard of the property were set off the road was a large white house, an unpainted wooden barn, a watering trough for horses, a grinding wheel, pasture, a rather large vegetable garden, a free-flowing spring, a chicken coop, and old maple trees. Chickens could be heard clucking about the barnyard all day long.

The inside of their farmhouse was furnished with fine furniture brought from Neville Island. I remember as a child seeing the beautiful parlor (that is what folks called living rooms then), furniture, and a piano. Grandma played piano. The furniture was purchased as a wedding present for my grandmother in 1901. She was about twenty years old at the time. Grandpa Cole was two years older. We have in our Melbourne home the sofa, armchair, and rocking chair from that parlor set. Years ago, my wife Carol had the rocker from the set reupholstered. My sister, Darlene, who inherited two pieces from the set, had them reupholstered.

Later, she gave her two pieces to Carol and me. As was the rule with my grandmother, a severe tongue-lashing befell any child of mine who dared sit on the ancient pieces of furniture. The three-piece set now enjoys a prominent place in our home.

I have many fond memories of my grandmother, Helen (Henderson) Cole. Many of those memories were visits to the Cole farm outside Sandy Lake, Pennsylvania. I remember the rather large kitchen where Grandma had both a gas stove and a cast iron coal-fired stove. Mostly, she cooked on the coal- fired stove. I remember her cooking for us children the best, quite soft gingerbread and sugar cookies I ever ate. She always served them with a glass of cold milk. Next to her house was a large vegetable garden. I remember seeing her in the garden hoeing the weeds away. She canned enough food from her garden to feed her family for most of the winter.

When I was about six or seven years old, Grandpa Cole left his farm and moved in with us at our little 736 McCalmont Street house. He stayed with us for less than six months. I sensed at the time that Grandpa had had a serious falling out with his oldest son, Robert. Grandpa and I slept in the same small room just off our living room. Grandpa, my several teddy bears, and I would crowd into my small bed. I remember Grandpa telling me many stories. Sadly, I forgot most of them and had to rely on my dad and my cousin, Marion, to fill in the many blanks in my memory.

After Grandpa turned the Sandy Lake farm over to his oldest son, Robert, Grandpa and Grandma Cole moved in with us at our new house at 805 McCalmont Street, Rocky Grove, Pennsylvania. When my dad built the house, he included on the second floor a small sitting room along with two bedrooms and a full bath. My grandmother kept her pedal-operated Singer sewing machine in her sitting room. Later, my dad changed the sitting room to a small kitchen and rented the apartment to high school teachers. When I was about twelve years old, Grandma taught me how to operate her Singer pedal sewing machine. She also taught me how to hook a rug. I managed to make one small rug. Somewhere along the road of our many moves, the little (not-quite-finished) rug got lost. These days, I have an old electric sewing machine that I occasionally use. My wife has a fancy electric Singer. Carol cringes if I touch her Singer. After a few years, Grandma and Grandpa moved from Rocky Grove to Syracuse, New York, to live with their oldest daughter, Gladys Bernhoft. I remember seeing Grandma Cole hoeing weeds in her small vegetable garden behind Aunt Gladys's house. I can also see

Grandma in my mind standing at the kitchen sink washing dishes. Grandpa died in Syracuse. After Aunt Gladys's husband, Arthur, died, Gladys moved to Kissimmee, Florida, and became a practical nurse. Grandma Cole moved in with Gladys. Grandma, in very frail condition, asked to be flown home to Pennsylvania. She died shortly after arriving in Pennsylvania. My grandpa died at eighty-nine years old. My grandma was ninety-seven.

One other memory of the farm at Sandy Lake comes to my mind. When I was about four or five years old I would sit on Grandpa's knee and look across the room at and old pendulum clock. One day my grandfather told me the if I could tell the time on the clock, he would give me one dollar. I got busy. With in a week, I proudly collected the dollar.

I have always loved watches with hands on their face. I often joked about digital watches by telling people, "If God had intended folks to tell time digitally, he would not have put hands on clocks."

CHAPTER 3

Grandma and Grandma Murrin's Story

Mom's father, James Henry Murrin, was born in Murrysville, Pennsylvania, on February 2, 1884. He died in Pittsburgh, Pennsylvania, on September 1952 when I was only a lad of twelve. James's friends called him Harry. His family simply addressed him as Pap. I remember Grandpa Murrin well. Pap Murrin was believed to be a descendant of a Revolutionary War Irishman by the name of Hugh Murrin. Hugh was born in Londonderry, Ireland, in 1749. From Ireland, he immigrated to America before the Revolutionary War. In 1799, he and his family moved to Butler County, Pennsylvania, to a wilderness area later named Murrinsville. There, he acquired four hundred acres, which he cleared and farmed until his death on October 27, 1841. In the town's cemetery lies a tombstone with his name and a reference to his Revolutionary War service. Hugh Murrin served in a Pennsylvania Revolutionary War unit until 1783. For his service, he was awarded two hundred acres in 1786, most likely in the Murrinsville, Pennsylvania, area. Murrinsville grew into a small town with a Catholic church, a small store, other buildings, and several houses. Hugh Murrin donated land for the church. When I was dating Carol, I passed along Route 308 through Murrinsville many times on my way between our two homes.

Grandpa Murrin was able to hold down a job all during the Great Depression of the 1930s. He worked as the general maintenance man at a Catholic facility run by Catholic nuns. The job paid low wages, but Grandpa was able to provide enough for his family so that his family was better off than most. I remember my mother telling me that often Grandma Murrin would share their meager food with less-fortunate, hungry neighbors.

I clearly remember when Grandpa Murrin died. I was just a little kid. What I remember most is the saddened silence of my mother and father. I remember the sadness of the funeral services held in Pittsburgh a few days after he died.

My Grandmother Murrin was born Lena Litt on November 29, 1890, to a Luxembourg (Germany) Catholic mother and father. I remember that one could make my grandma very angry if one was dumb enough to speak her name and German in the same breath. She would loudly correct you by stating that she was a Luxembourger! The Luxembourg family immigrated to America in about 1890 and settled into a farmer's life in Minnesota. I once met my Great-grandmother Litt when our family vacationed by train to Minnesota about 1948. I was just a small boy. I remember a big white house and dairy barn with a large front yard with several large old trees. My great- grandmother, Anna Koenig (Pleats) Litt, was born in Luxembourg on May 1, 1870. She became a naturalized citizen in Winona, Minnesota, a few years after her arrival. She died March 27, 1953. My great-grandfather, Herbert Litt, was also born in Luxembourg. In 1857, he immigrated to Minnesota in 1890. He died in 1925. Herbert became a naturalized citizen at the same place as my great-grandmother and probably at the same time. I am not certain if they were married before or after they immigrated. Given that my Grandmother Murrin was born in 1891 in Minnesota, evidence suggests that Anna and Herbert were married in Luxembourg before they immigrated. Grandma Murrin had three sisters, Katheryn, Clara, and Emma. Grandma Murrin died on January 19, 1976. I was twenty-five years old at the time and still on active duty in the air force.

When I was about eight years old, my mother and two sisters, Darlene and Evelyn, traveled by train to Minnesota a few weeks earlier than my dad and me. My dad only got two weeks of vacation a year. Dad left me in the care of my aunt and Uncle Cole at their Sandy Lake farm. I was utterly miserable. I missed my momma. When Dad and I finally arrived in Minnesota, I remember running up to my mother, hugging her leg, and telling her that I would never leave her again.

My mom was an avid movie fan. When my two sisters and I were little kids, our mom would walk us about three blocks to a bus stop for a ride into the town of Franklin about one and a half miles away. I never remember my mother did not drive an automobile. She did learn to drive, but after her first husband was killed in an automobile accident she never drove again.

Mom regularly took us to the Kayton Theater located on Liberty Avenue at the lower end of town. My mom loved musicals, so mostly that is what we saw. As a little kid, I was not a big fan of musicals, but I loved the Mickey Mouse and Donald Duck cartoons. The newsreels were of interest to me too. The cartoons were, by far, my favorites.

In downtown Franklin, a short block away on the same street was another movie theater called the Orpheum. The Orpheum played B Westerns and war movies. My friend, Roy Shingledecker, and I saw many fifteen-cent movies at the Orpheum. As kids, Roy and I watched a classic movie, *High Noon*, starring Gary Cooper. We thought by the title that we were about to watch a war movie. It turned out to be a classic Western. Even at the time as young kids, we knew the movie would become a classic. The tune from the movie still rings in my head: "Oh, my darling, do not forsake me on this our wedding day ..."

I remember visiting Grandpa and Grandma Murrin's home on Spring Garden Avenue, a bedroom community on the fringe of the city of Pittsburgh. I recall that at that time, their house did not have a bathtub or a shower. Our mothers would give us little kids a bath in the kitchen sink. I remember one time while the older folks were in the house's central room talking, I climbed up a tall, white, metal cabinet in Grandma's kitchen. I made it to the top shelf all right, but over the cabinet came. We both crashed to the kitchen floor. I do not remember Grandma Murrin ever saying an unkind word to me about the incident.

For many years before Grandpa Murrin died, the Pittsburgh clan, including Grandma Murrin, would motor to our home in Rocky Grove for a Thanksgiving dinner. I have many fond memories of those dinners and can yet in my mind's eye see all my relatives around a large table in our basement. I have 8mm files of those times so can relive them any time I feel nostalgic.

Grandma Murrin was a big-hearted, independent person. She insisted on living in her own house on Spring Garden Avenue after Grandpa Murrin died.

For much of the time she lived there, she took in a handicapped older woman named Henrietta. Grandma stayed in that house until she died in 1976.

I remember many summer days spent at Grandma Murrin's house climbing the steep slope behind her house and exploring the thin forest surrounding the area.

CHAPTER 4

My Mother and Father's Story

My father clearly remembered his home on Neville Island, the farm, the factory, the school he attended, the farmhands, the horses and mules, and many of his farmer neighbors. Dad was born Ned M. Cole on March 21, 1911, on Neville Island. Dad inherited his mother's large ears and, from somewhere in his lineage, bowlegs and flat feet. My dad passed the big ears on to me and my sister, Darlene. The flat feet kept him out of the military.

My father was an optimistic man, but he clearly remembered the fear that surrounded his island family. In his later life, my father chose not to dwell on the times of fear, but instead focused his mind on his good memories of his island home. Many years later, toward the end of my father's life, my wife, my dad, my two sisters, and two of cousins visited the island. The gate to the old cemetery was locked. Not to be deterred, we climbed over the gate. What a thrill it was for me to observe seeing my dad revel in the sights and long silent sounds he remembered so well as we walked around the island.

Life on the Sandy Lake farm was arduous work for my father. Many times as a child, we visited the Sandy Lake farm. My father and his older brother, Robert, did not get along well. My dad told me that he and his brother fought often. My dad, who was younger and smaller, got much the worse of the brawls. By the time my father was a teenager, he had toughened up quite a lot. He and his brother got into a knockdown, dragged-out fistfight in the lower section of their barn. It must have been quite a fight. On the occasion of this fistfight with his brother, my dad gave more than he got. The two brothers never fought again.

Life on the farm was not all misery for my dad. On my dad's sixteenth birthday, his father purchased a new automobile, which he permitted my father to drive. His Uncle Frank presented him with a 25-caliber semi-automatic Colt which my father handed down in a roundabout way.

My dad offered his prized possession, the 25 Colt, to a dear boyhood friend, Glenn Heasley, who drove a bus during the Great Depression. One day, Glenn approached Dad and asked him if he had a weapon that he could loan him for self-protection while he drove his bus. Typical of my dad, he gave to Glenn his prized possession the 25-caliber Colt. My dad told Glenn that he would not sell him the gun, but if ever Glenn no longer needed it, my dad would buy it back from him. Many years later, Glenn came to the old Cole farm on the occasion of my Grandmother Cole's death in 1976. I was able to talk with Glenn and brought up the subject of the Colt. Glenn told my dad and me that he would be back the next day with the gun. And he did return with the weapon with the original bullets in hand. Glenn said to me that he could not directly hand the gun to me, but felt honor bound to return it to my dad's hand, and so he did. My dad handed the weapon to me. I have since passed the Colt on to my wife for her personal protection. One of these days, Carol will pass it on to one of my children or grandchildren. Hopefully, the Colt will stay in the family for many generations.

My dad purchased an Indian-brand motorcycle while still in high school. Finishing high school was not high on my dad's priorities. After the second or third time as a high school senior, my dad was sitting in school beside an open springtime window. In those days, air-conditioning was still many years in the future. Outside his window came one of his friends on a motorcycle. The friend whispered his plans to take off for Texas. My dad glanced out the window at his friend and back at the teacher. The friend and his motorcycle won out. Out the window, my dad jumped. He never returned to high school. Off to Texas they went.

Backing up a bit when Dad was a young guy. I think this was before he took off for Texas. Dad came back home, but took off for Texas again later. In any event, Dad and some friends were out on an automobile joyride. Dad was riding in the rumble seat of the car. The car was in a serious wreck. My dad was badly injured. His pelvis bone was crushed, as were several other bones. Dad spent a month or so in a hospital recovering from the injuries but managed to survive into his late 80's.

I remember my dad telling me that one of his backbreaking jobs on the farm was weeding the rows and rows of asparagus located along the dirt road leading to Sandy Lake. My dad told me that one day, he got to the end of his row after an hour or so toiling under a sweltering summer sun. He just could not do it anymore. So off he ran to Texas. My dad was really not a fan of backbreaking farm work.

As an aside, the Cole farm also had a large orchard of apple trees. They harvested the apples and trucked them off to Pittsburgh. Originally, they sorted and packed the apples by hand. My dad, along with field hands, picked many bushels of apples. At some time, I think before I was born, the family built a building, which housed apple sorting machinery. I remember watching the machine do its job. I was just a little kid. My grandpa would let us eat all the apples we wanted. To this day, I love red, delicious apples.

So back to the Texas odyssey. On one of his motorcycle trips to Texas, my dad and his buddy came upon a small Southern town. (The time was during the Great Depression.) They were stopped at the outskirts of town by the town sheriff. He hauled them off to jail for being vagrants. They were thrown in a cell with another fellow. My dad and his friend were cold, tired, hungry, and broke.

The cellmate made them an offer. The cellmate suggested that they could earn one dollar if they would do a number on the cellmate's lower parts. My dad and his friend debated the issue quietly between themselves. They decided that they were not that hungry. The next morning at dawn, the sheriff escorted them to the south end of town and turned them loose.

When they arrived in Longview, Texas, my dad got a job working as a ranch hand on a Texas ranch. My dad was quite a personable fellow and soon became well-liked by the ranch family. The rancher had a young and quite pretty daughter with whom my dad became quite stricken, and the girl with him. Soon, wedding plans were in full motion. On the wedding day, my dad got cold feet, jumped on his motorcycle, and took off. He never saw the girl again. In the telling of the story, I could tell that in my dad's mind, the whole sordid affair was not one of his proudest moments. Many years later, his stood-up fiancée managed to contact my dad after her husband died. I guess she got over being mad at him.

Many years later, I happened to be passing through Longview, Texas. I could not resist making up a tale that I was sure would turn my dad's face red. I told my dad that upon passing through Longview, I stopped at a diner for a bite to eat. I told him that I sat down next to an old gentleman and began a conversation. The old guy asked me where I was from and what was my name. When I told him Pennsylvania and my name was Ned M. Cole Jr., the old guy jumped up from his seat, got right in my face, and said, "You tell that son-of-a-bitch father of yours that I hope he rots in hell." My dad's face turned fire red. I could not help but break out in a belly-bouncing laugh. My dad, who always had a great sense of humor, started to laugh too, but then sheepishly asked me, "Did that really happen?"

On one of Dad's jaunts to Texas, the Indian motorcycle comes back into the story. An acquaintance of my dad kept pressing my dad to sell him the motorcycle. Because the motorcycle was my dad's only means of transportation, he was understandably not interested in selling the machine. One day, his acquaintance asked my dad if he could at least take the bike for a ride. So my dad, being the nice guy that he was, said, "Ok." That was the last he ever saw of the guy or the motorcycle.

My dad returned home to Sandy Lake, Pennsylvania. Times were still difficult in the United States and around the world. The Great Depression continued to make finding a job difficult. My dad took the only job he could find. He spent the next few months cracking stones for highways. Lucky for him, Dad was always in great shape. Although the job was backbreaking, Dad cracked rocks with the best of the crew. One day, one of Dad's fellow workers fell behind in making his rock-cracking quota. Dad had already filled his quota, so he started to help his fellow worker who had fallen behind. The foreman noticed what my dad was doing and ordered him to stop. He shouted at my dad, "If a man cannot pull his own weight, he does not belong on my crew." The older, slower man was dismissed. My dad never knew what happened to the poor fellow.

Soon thereafter, my dad and a couple of his friends leased an abandoned coal mine. They shored up the mine ceiling and walls and dug ever deeper, into the dark earth. Outside the mine, the coal miners lived in a shack of a place. One evening, my dad and his friends were sitting around playing cards when my dad announced that it was time that the other miners cleaned themselves up a bit and at the least combed their hair once in a while. Dad pulled out his Colt 38 special (the same Colt that his father had carried to Mexico) and ordered one of the guys to stand against the wall of the shack. Dad then fired one shot right at the top of the guy's head, parting his hair. At least the guy looked a little neater.

The mine prospered. Dad and his friends were making a decent living. But then lease renewal came up and the owner of the land refused to renew the lease. The owner took over the now functioning mine himself. My dad and his friends were out of work again. Franklin Roosevelt was elected to his second term as president. Hitler was rising to power in Europe.

Dad moved to Pittsburgh, Pennsylvania, where he got a job as a field hand at a place called Dixmont. Having worked on a farm much of his life, Dad could handle plow horses well. While working at Dixmont and living nearby, Dad met my mother, Anna Eveline Murrin, a good Catholic from a good Catholic family. They were married July 17, 1939, in Sandy Lake, Pennsylvania.

From the time that I was a little kid, my dad managed to have at least some type of boat. The first boat I remember was a green metal rowboat. Dad took our family many times to small lakes and rivers around Rocky Grove to fish, swim, boat, and camp. Later on, when Mom and Dad did not have to spend all their money on us kids, my dad bought a powerboat. He water-skied into his eighties.

My dad often claimed that there was Native American in his family line. His mother adamantly denied the claim. One of the Bragdon daughter was captured by Native Americans. When she returned home, she was pregnant with an Indian baby. So my dad was right in claiming Indian blood.

Evelyn, my mother, was born Anna Eveline Murrin on March 22, 1919, in Murrinsville, Pennsylvania, to a German Irish Catholic mother and father, James Henry Murrin and Lena (Litt) Murrin.

Mom went by the name Evelyn all her life even though that was not her exact birth name. My mother had a rather tragic life. Her first husband, Eugene Cassidy, was killed in an automobile accident. Mom was left with a small child, my sister, Evelyn Bernice Cassidy (later formally adopted by my father to become Evelyn Bernice Cole). Mom was a consummate, stay-at- home mother. The love I felt for my mom from the day I was born until this day knows no limits. Mom was a very vigorous lady of some notoriety in our small community for her many contributing works for the Rocky Grove Volunteer Fire Department. Mom pretty much ran the ladies auxiliary. Taking after her mother, Lena (Litt) Murrin, Mom was quite a hard-headed German (sorry, Grandma, Luxembourger). For her community contributions, Mom was named "Woman of the

Year" for her small community. Later, my sister, Evelyn (Cole) Karns, was also named "Woman of the Year" for much the same work. To this very day in her eighties, my sister stays involved in the Rocky Grove Volunteer Fire Department.

When Mom was young, she had some rather severe knee problems. They called her knee malady in those days "water on the knee." When Darlene and I were young and did naughty things (of course, not me, I was an angel, but Darlene, I must confess was at times somewhat of a devil), Mom would chase us around our little house with a switch. Seldom with her stiff knee was she never able to catch us.

At age fifty-four, Mom had a stroke in Franklin Hospital while recovering from a gall bladder operation. To this day, I am convinced that the stroke was caused by a mistake by the anesthesiologist. Our family was not the suing type, so nothing was ever done about it. My mom spent the rest of her life partly blind and paralyzed on one side. The burden of her care fell upon my father. My dad passed away from pancreatic cancer in August 1998. My mom died of a saddened heart just a few months later. Both spent their final days in the Sugarcreek Manor nursing home.

My mother had two sisters (Mary and Helen) and one brother (Charles). She had other siblings who did not survive into adulthood. Mary was born July 2, 1922. Helen was born a year or so earlier. Uncle Chuck was born about 1925. Chuck served in the United States Navy during World War II. He managed to survive a ship that was sunk by a typhoon. When my Uncle Chuck returned from the war, he married Agnus, a quite pretty, blond-haired, young woman. Sadly, for Aunt Agnus, Uncle Chuck died when he was fifty- nine years old of a heart attack.

Aunt Mary was my favorite aunt. Aunt Mary and her children spent many days at our home on Mccalmont Street, Rocky Grove, Pennsylvania.

My mother and my siblings spent many days visiting Aunt Mary at her home in Shaler Township, a suburb of Pittsburgh, Pennsylvania. Aunt Mary was a good dancer. Whenever we had the opportunity, Aunt Mary and I cut quite a jig dancing the polka. Even when Aunt Mary was on oxygen, we managed to get in a few steps. Aunt Mary died when I was working in China. To my great regret, I was not able to attend her funeral services. I remember so many days when Aunt Mary visited our home. I especially remember sitting around the dinner table when I was just a kid listening to adults talk. My aunt really enjoyed pulling my dad's leg. She could make my dad's face turn fire red when she let loose with a few good curse words. My dad really liked Aunt Mary and I believe enjoyed her teasing him. My mother and Aunt Mary were lifelong friends.

One day, not long before my dad died, I told him that he could teach me one more thing. He asked what that might be. I asked him if he could teach me how to die with dignity. That he did. The last time I saw my dad standing was at the Sugarcreek Nursing Home. As I got up to leave, my dad said to me, "Hold on a minute." By then, Dad was in great pain. He slowly rose from his wheelchair, stood as straight as he could manage, and took a faltering step toward me. He stuck out his hand. Shaking hands had always been our tradition when me met and parted. I cry as I write these words of honor about my father.

I was fortunate enough to be at my dad's bedside when he died. I remember holding his hand and quietly talking to him. With his last breath, I heard him whisper, "Mom, I am coming." With that, he stopped breathing. A staff nurse informed me that Dad was gone. I said, "No, not yet." I placed my hand on his neck and felt his heartbeat slowly ebb away. When the beat stopped, I said, "Now, he is gone." I very much cherish the thought that I was able to enjoy the life of my dad until the very end.

In my mother's case, I walked into her nursing home room just a few minutes after my mother died. Sitting beside her bed was my ever-faithful sister, Snooky. She looked up at me with tears in her eyes and told me that Mom was gone. My mother died in late 1998 just a few months after my dad passed away in August.

After my dad died, my mom told us kids many times that she just did not want to live anymore. She willed herself to be with my dad.

I spoke these words of memorial at my mother's funeral. For reasons I, to this day, do not understand, I was unable to find in my mind any words to say at my dad's funeral service.

The three of us, Evelyn Karns, Ned Cole, and Darlene Coberly, the children of Ned and Evelyn Cole, stood before you just four months ago to give tribute to our father. Now, we are here to say our last goodbyes to our mother.

Our mom has had a great struggle for most of her eighty years.

She was born March 27, 1919, Anna Eveline Murrin to a German mother and Irish father at a spot not far from where we now stand. She was baptized Roman Catholic. In June 1936, she married Gene Cassidy. In August 1937, Evelyn Cassidy, our sister, known to you as Snooky Karns, was born to the couple when my mother was eighteen years old. Our mom stood beside helplessly as her husband, Gene Cassidy, was struck down by an automobile on the streets of Pittsburgh in 1939. She began a new life with our dad, Ned Cole. At the age of fifty-four years when most of us begin to look forward to the quiet peace of retirement, our mom suffered a stroke, which left her partly blind and partly an invalid. For the last four years of her life, she was confined to a wheelchair and a nursing home. Yet, working together with love and care, our mom and dad did not give up twenty-five years ago. Instead, they went on to enjoy life as best they could together. They did their very best not to pass on to us the burdens of their lives. But, for us children, we will always feel the deep pain of knowing that our mom and dad had to suffer far beyond that which most could bear. With all the burdens they had to carry, never once did they ever stop showing love and kindness to us, their children. To their children, the gift of unconditional love was a blessing all of our lives.

But today, we are not here to tell you the story of the life of our mom and dad together, or our lives with them, but rather we are here to tell you the story of the unbounded love our mom gave us from the time we were little children, through the troubles of growing up, and on through the difficult years of our mom's own life.

Each day of our lives was always Mother's Day to us. We remember as though all those Mother's Days are yet today.

Each of us remembers the gentleness with which you, Mom, dressed us when we were little and made us feel proud of how we looked.

Each of us remembers the many times when you gently nursed us when we were sick. You never forgot our birthdays. You made each of us feel special on our special day.

We remember we were not afraid at night because each night, you tucked us in and kissed us into our dreams. We always slept the sleep of trusting little kids because we knew that you were there to protect us.

We remember the Easters when you dressed us and held our hand on the way to church. We remember so proudly thinking, "Isn't she so pretty? She is our mom."

We remember how proud you made us feel when we came home from school, we showed you our report cards. She never said an unkind word no matter the grades. You just smiled, gave us a hug, and told us how proud she was that she had such good kids.

In and out of school, you made us believe in ourselves because unconditionally, you were proud of us in things big and small.

Now, when we look back on those times, we know of the many sacrifices you made to make our lives better.

Each of us remembers the unconditional acceptance and love you extended to us when we married, when there were troubles in our marriages, when we brought into our family children of other races, and at all the other times of our trials.

We remember the unconditional forgiveness and unconditional love you showed us during those times when our deeds could have been better.

But mostly, Mom, we each remember that from our first memories as tiny tots until the last day of your life, we each knew in our hearts that you loved us without bounds for just being as we are.

Never can we measure how much that love has meant to each of us. Mom, it is still with great pride and love that we say, "This is our mom." Know that we loved you too.

Darlene and I had somewhat different memories of our childhood at 736 McCalmont Street, especially of our mother. I am not saying that Darlene and I argued about our memories of our mom. We just remember things a bit differently. For me, childhood was idyllic and very happy.

My mom and dad at first lived with Grandma and Grandpa Murrin in a house on Troy Hill, a suburb of Pittsburgh, Pennsylvania. I was born on April 1, 1940, in St John's Hospital, Pittsburgh, Pennsylvania. Go, Steelers. When I was a year and a half old, my dad got a job on the Pennsylvania Railroad. He stayed with the railroad until he retired on March 31, 1976, as a freight train conductor. On the very next day, the Pennsylvania Railroad became Conrail. The Pennsylvania Railroad passed into the annuals of history.

The family moved to 736 McCalmont Street, Rocky Grove, Pennsylvania, a bedroom suburb of Franklin, Pennsylvania. The house was a little two- bedroom bungalow. The house was on the lower side of the street. The road in front of the house was dirt covered as was the ditch which ran the length of the lot. In the back of the house was a detached garage and a plot for gardening. In the front of the yard were, what seemed to me as little kid, two giant maple trees. One had no branches close to the ground. A second tree had one low- hanging branch. The low-branch tree was great for climbing.

Many summers I spent happily playing with my cars and trucks in the dirt ditch in front of the house. When I was nine or ten years old, a family named Lesh moved in across our street. The oldest girl was named Linda. I thought that she was the prettiest girl I had ever seen. Being somewhat bashful at the time, I never did get around to making an overt courting approach to Linda. Linda moved away and we both moved on with our lives.

In 1951, my dad bought a piece of land a block and a half north on McCalmont Street. There, he built a very nice two-story house with his own hands. How my dad did it, we still marvel at to this day. My dad's railroad job kept him away several days at a time. Then, he would be home for a couple of days. On his days off Dad come home, change into his work clothes and work on building our house. He would often work late into the night. By midnight lights would still be blazing.

Dad would get a call from the railroad advising him to report to work in an hour or so. Dad would tell my mom to let him sleep for fifteen minutes, wake him up, and send him off to his railroad job. Dad was the hardest working man I ever knew. I like to think, "Like father, like son."

All of the lumber for Dad's new house we purchased from the Crum lumber mill. The mill was just a block away from our new homesite at 805 McCalmont Street. Mr. Crum was kind enough to permit my dad and me to plane all the lumber in his mill. The two-by-fours, one-by-fours, and two-by-sixes we would plane only on the narrow edge. So, my dad's whole house was built with thicker than normal siding, studs, and rafters.

My dad was a man of great honor and integrity. He was a kind man who helped many people less blessed than he. Dad was a neat freak regarding his person and clothing, to put it mildly. He pressed his own pants with a crease so sharp, one could cut a hardwood log. Dad had a great sense of humor, but I suspect like all of us, he used humor to hide his own self-doubts about himself. He was quite bowlegged and had inherited outsized ears from his mother. No doubt the bowlegs and big ears were a source of hidden chagrin to my dad. Yet, Dad always could take a practical joke played on him with good humor.

I quite remember one time my dad, my brother-in-law, Pat Karns, and I were camping and boating at Tionesta Dam. Late in the evening as we sat around our campfire, we started to tell stories of snakes and bears which heavily populated that area of Pennsylvania. I excused myself for a few moments and slipped into our tent, whereupon I slipped a rope inside my dad's sleeping bag. Soon, we retired for the night.

When I figured that my dad was asleep, I slowly began to draw the rope out of my dad's sleeping bag. My dad came fully awake and said in a startled voice, "Oh! Oh! Oh!" and leaped from his sleeping bag. Pat and I could not stop laughing. My dad got the joke and laughed heartily along with Pat and me. That was my dad.

My father and I worked a great deal together. He instilled in me from an early age the Puritan ethic of hard work. I remember one day Dad and I drove his 1947 pickup truck to the village cincer pile. In these days the ashes were free to anyone. We filled the bed of his pickup and drove back hoke and proceeded to spread the ashes on the dirt road which ran all along the found of our house. My dad and I always had a bit of a work contest between us back home, and proceeded to spread the as Each of us shoveled the ashes out of the truck at a furious rate. Later, my dad and I painted many houses during the summer idle times, which always befell railroad workers. A friend of my dad's Clyde Anthony, a fellow railroad worker, often painted with us. Clyde and I would often get into a painting speed contest. Clyde, to his embarrassment, could never keep up with me. Much later, my boss at ABC Rail Corporation, Glenn Stinson, once introduced me to another fellow as the hardest worker he had ever known. My dad would have been proud.

I have very loving memories of my dad, but also to this day, I view some of his trepidations with anguish. Dad was raised in a strict Protestant tradition led by his very religious mother. Dad held in his mind a healthy dose of argument for anyone who would challenge his religious beliefs. This is not to say that Dad harped on us kids about religion. He did not. I clearly recall one day when Dad and I were working on Dad's Christmas tree farm. I had just finished my second year of college and, as nearly all young folks, had a lot of questions in my mind. I happened to bring up the subject of religion. I made the mistake of relating to Dad that I had some misgivings. My dad, in a harsh voice, advised me in no uncertain terms that I was forbidden to ever speak in such terms again. That was the very last time I ever brought up the subject of religion with my dad. Later, when I and my two sisters, let's say, strayed from the religious fold, my dad would ask Darlene and I where he went wrong. I never had the courage to tell him that it was his intolerance.

CHAPTER 5

My Sister Snooky's Story

Evelyn (lovingly called "Snooky" by all who know her), my oldest sister, was born on January 12, 1944, to Anna Eveline (Murrin) Cassidy and her first husband, a Mr. Cassidy. (Mom was never called by her real name. Everyone just called her Ev.)

Not long after Snooky was born, my mom's first husband was killed in an automobile accident. In about 1938, my dad met my mom when my dad worked in the Pittsburgh area. In 1938, they were married. Snooky was quite an attractive little girl. She grew up to be a varsity basketball cheerleader at our high school. After graduating from Rocky Grove High School in 1955, she attended and graduated from a secretarial school in Pittsburgh, Pennsylvania. Upon graduation, she got a job at Franklin Steel Company located in the eastern outskirts of Franklin, Pennsylvania. The plant back snuggled up against the north bank of French Creek.

Not long after she started working, she met Patrick Karns, a handsome young fellow just a few years older. Snooky and Pat were married on June 9, 1957. Snooky and Pat remained married and live in the same house they moved into after a short stay in another house. The house was built to Pat's specifications and remodeled several times over the years. Snooky and Pat's first of four children, Michael Karns, was born in September 1958. At the time, I was a first-year student at Pennsylvania State University. I remember well the phone call I received telling me that I was an uncle.

Snooky deserved far better than I once treated her. She was home from school with an illness. I was tasked with bringing her a glass of water whenever she demanded. I decided that I was not her slave, so when she demanded water for what seemed like the millionth time, I dipped a glass of water out of our toilet. I only told her where it came from after she drank it. Snooky forgave me, of course. That was the way she was. Had the event been reversed, I doubt if I would have ever been so forgiving. I was about six years old at the time. I am truly sorry, Snooky.

Michael was blessed with two brothers and a sister: David, Tom, and Cindy. David Karns went on to a successful US Navy career. Tom is now a successful electrician. Tom and his wife and kids live in the Franklin area. Cindy married not long after graduating from Rocky Grove High School, and now lives with her husband and kids near Erie Pennsylvania., Pennsylvania.

Snooky became very active in the Rocky Grove Volunteer Fire Department's Lady Auxiliary. For years, like her mother, she was the head chef for the many RGFD Auxiliary functions. Like her mother, Snooky was named Rocky Grove's Woman of the Year. Her kids and grandkids still live in the area and continue the fire department tradition of the Karns tribe.

When Snooky's kids were no longer underfoot, she started to work at a local greenhouse. She became a very talented flower arrangement specialist. Snooky worked not because she needed to. Her husband provided well for his family. Snooky just liked to work. Following many years working at a floral greenhouse, Snooky was hired as head chef at a local nursing home. My mother and father both spent the end of their days on earth in that same nursing home. Snooky visited them every day at the end of her shift. She was by their bedsides when they died.

There will never be another Snooky. She can talk one's leg off with her encyclopedic knowledge of the people and goings-on in her small community. Snooky is an endlessly kind person with a pure heart of gold. To know Snooky is to love her. The world will be a sad place when she passes on to her just reward.

CHAPTER 6

Ned M. Cole Jr.'s Story

I, Ned M. Cole Jr., was born April 1, 1940, at 4:10 PM to Ned M. Cole and Evelyn (Murrin) Cole in St. John's Hospital, Pittsburgh, Pennsylvania. Early on, because he was named after his father, he was nicknamed "Tuck." Most of his family still call him by his nickname.

I take great pride in my family's long history of military service. My forefathers served and fought for America in almost every war since our Revolution War. My great-grandfathers, cousins, and uncles served or fought throughout the history of our nation. Some died in service to protect our freedoms. I served in the United States Air Force, Pennsylvania ANG, and New York ANG for nearly all of my adult life.

I trace much of my lineage to the British Islands. And until recently, I have been proud of that lineage. But, when the British government refused to grant asylum to a Christian lady held for years in a Pakistani prison for daring to give water to a Muslim woman, I felt ashamed of my British heritage… Hopefully, the United States government will not be so coldhearted.

My first home was on Troy Hill, a section of Pittsburgh, Pennsylvania. The house was owned or rented by my Grandmother and Grandfather Murrin. I have no early memory of that house, but I have visited it a number of times, so I have the look of the house firmly planted in my mind.

At the time I was born, my dad worked at a place called Dixmont. I remember Dad telling me that he was hired because of his farming experience and was quite experienced in working behind a horse and plow. My dad told me that he was out in a field with his horse and plow when he got word that I had been born. He unharnessed the horse, jumped on the horse's bare back, and raced back to the barn. When he got to the hospital, he was told that he had a son. Because the day was April 1, both he and my mom thought the boy part was an April Fools' joke. Not so. My mother insisted that I be named after my father.

When I was one and a half years old, my mother and dad moved from Troy Hill to a small rental place outside Sandy Lake, Pennsylvania. Not long after, they moved to a little suburb of Franklin, Pennsylvania, called Rocky Grove. At the time, Rocky Grove had a population of about five thousand. Franklin's population was about ten thousand. My dad got a job as a trainman for the Pennsylvania Railroad, where he worked until he retired in 1976. Dad spent many overnights riding the rails from Oil City, Pennsylvania, to Buffalo, New York.

Our little house was at 736 McCalmont Street. The dirt road in front of the house years ago gave way to asphalt. I can still see clearly in my mind my sister's bedroom, Mom and Dad's bedroom, a small kitchen with its "icebox" and its large fin cooler atop, a central room where we watched television and played games, a living room, and a small dayroom. The dayroom eventually became my bedroom. The dirt road at the front of the house was often treated with sticky oil to keep down dust. So that we could cross the road to our neighbors without getting our bare feet all sticky with tar, we would make little paths with dirt across the road.

I can still see in my mind the fine, old maple trees standing in our front yard. The trees are gone now.

Next door to our house were three vacant lots. The lots made a fine baseball field for the children of our neighborhood. We kept the lots mowed and built a chicken-wire backstop. For many summers, we kids played ball on that field. There were not enough boys, so the girls got to play too.

Not infrequently, one of us would foul off a ball and break one of my dad's windows. I never recall my dad punishing us for breaking his window. He just fixed the window.

In the back of the property was a detached garage where my dad kept his 1936 Ford. Next to and back of the garage was a garden plot. I remember many summers spading the plot, planting vegetables, and weeding what seemed to me at the time a very large garden. The plot was probably no more than five thousand square feet. Weeding the garden was not my favorite chore.

Directly behind the house was a small yard and a doghouse. When we children were little, my dad built a swing set out of two-inch steel pipes. The swing set had a swing, two swing bars, a seesaw, and a porch swing. Many neighborhood kids came to play on the swing set. My sister, Darlene, and I charged the neighborhood kids one leaf to take turns riding our swing set. Years later, I built a similar swing set for my children.

When my dad was on the railroad going from Oil City, Pennsylvania, to Buffalo, New York, he often passed an Indian reservation. Indian dogs would run by Dad's slow-moving train. Dad and his trainmen would toss chunks of food out to the dogs. One dog figured out that competition was light on the other side of the train, so it would run under the train to get his treats. The next trip or so, the train stopped to take on water and fuel at the Indian reservation. My dad jumped off and convinced one of the Indians to sell him the dog for two dollars. He brought the dog home and named him Brownie. That dog loved my dad. We always knew when Dad was coming home from work. Brownie would start barking as soon as my dad's old Ford turned the corner about a block away. Brownie was a great dog.

In the wintertime, many of we children would sled down McCalmont Street to our schoolhouse. In those days, the road was dirt and was not plowed or salted. Brownie would always go with me. There was no leash-your-dog rules in those days. Brownie would not ride the sled down the hill but would race alongside me. When we got to the bottom, I would harness Brownie up in a harness I had made, and he would pull the sled back up the hill. Almost every day, Brownie would follow me to school in the morning. When school let out in the afternoon, Brownie was always waiting for me at the back door of the school. . Sadly, when I was about ten years old, Brownie was playing ball with some children who lived on busy Rocky Grove Avenue. He raced out on the street to fetch a ball and was run over and killed by an automobile.

When I got a little older, my dad bought me a set of boxing gloves. My friend, Roy Shingledecker, and another neighborhood boy named Ron Cheers boxed many times in Dad's backyard. Roy and I were close to the same age. Ron was a couple of years older. I remember that I could beat Roy most of the time, and Roy could beat Ron. But Ron could beat me. Go figure.

One and a half blocks down McCalmont Street was Rocky Grove Grade and High School. Until I got out and about the world, I thought all children went to grade school and high school in the same building. We walked to school rain or shine, snowing or not. McCalmont Street was dirt its whole length to the school. Most of the kids walked to school. A few who lived more than a mile away rode a bus. At lunchtime, the walkers went home for lunch. My mom always had our lunch ready as soon as we got home. The bus-riding kids packed a brown bag lunch. The school had no cafeteria. We would hurry through lunch in good weather and hustle back to the school where many of the kids played softball. I remember one big guy named Bill Knapp who could hit a ball a mile. Not infrequently, he would hit the ball far enough to break a window on the back of the school's gymnasium.

The school had junior and senior varsity basketball teams, a track team, and a baseball team. We had no football team. I always regretted that I never got to play football. I was a poor basketball player and never made the varsity team. But I was named team equipment manager, so I got to ride a bus with the team to all away games. In my senior year, I turned over my equipment manager's job to a friend, Sam Gilmore. I felt sorry for Sam, who was a puny little guy but was very smart. Sam majored in physics at Penn State but chose for his lifework to be a minister.

I did excel at pole vaulting and set the school pole-vaulting record my senior year. My record lasted exactly one year when Flip Wile, a kid a year or two, younger than me whom I taught to pole-vault, broke my record.

At the time I was pole vaulting, I had a job at the A&P grocery store in Franklin, Pennsylvania. I would have to leave the track to go to work. The officials permitted me to take all my jumps and leave. I would never know until the next day whether I won or lost the meet.

The highlight of my pole-vaulting career occurred at a track meet held at the United States Military Academy at West Point. I was a freshman at Pennsylvania State University at the time. After the meet, on the bus ride back to Penn State, Coach Ingle asked me, "How did you do?" I answered, "I won." He retorted back, "How did you do"? I then understood and answered back, "Ten feet, six inches." To this day, I remember the lesson he taught me.

I recall my time growing up in Rocky Grove very warmly. I remember being a very happy little kid. School was not my favorite pastime, but playing with my friends and building things was a joy. A kid who lived across my street, David Carter, and another kid, Joe Neely, who lived a couple houses away, spent endless hours racing our bicycles all over the neighborhood, playing endless hours of cowboys and Indians, playing softball on the side lot beside my house, and hiking in the giant forest which started not a block away from my house. My favorite time was the summers. I recall one day in June when school was just off for the summer. Joe Neely and I lay at dusk in a neighbor's side yard looking up at a clear night sky. The day was balmy warm. Just perfect. I count that day with a beautiful night sky and a whole summer ahead to be one of the happiest days of my life.

As I grew into a young teenager, I began to build tree houses in the forest surrounding our community. My first tree house was built on a single-limb, an old oak tree about a half mile into the forest. About a quarter of a mile up a long slope, I located a small spring. From the spring, I laid old, abandoned oil well water pipes down the slope to my tree house. Using an old streetlight shade, I installed it as a sink into which I piped water. Because the tree house was built on a single limb, I used small tree logs to secure the tree house in place. One day, some destructive kids knocked the struts off. Down the tree house fell to the ground.

I decided to build an underground house located in a small meadow surrounded by thorn trees. I dug a sizable hole and entrance trench into the hole. Inside the hole, I built a small wooden structure. Over the trench, I built a roof so that I could crawl into my underground house. After I finished the underground structure, I covered the roof with sod and planted a small tree. The access tunnel which extended into the thorn trees was covered and sodded over. I nearly finished the tunnel covering when some hooligans discovered my nearly finished underground house and destroyed it.

Undeterred, I dragged lumber a mile or so into the forest and proceeded to build a second tree house. This time, I built the tree house high in an old oak tree and made a ten-foot ladder out of slender tree logs. Ten feet up the tree, I nailed short tree logs up the tree trunk to the tree house. Each evening when I would finish working, I would hide the ten-foot ladder some distance away from the tree where the tree house was built. As far as I know, the tree house lasted until the whole area was logged out.

The last tree house I built was near our house located at 805 McCalmont Street. It was quite an elaborate structure. My boyhood friends and I spent many nights sleeping over in the tree house. I remember one night when my friends and were sleeping over. We played penny ante poker and made a great deal of noise. My Father came up to the tree house and demanded that we all leave. I guess some neighbors complained. When I left home for college, my sister, Darlene, and her friends used the tree house as a neat hideout and to occasionally sleep over. The tree house lasted for many years until the fire department deemed it unsafe.

I am chagrined today to admit that as a kid, I played cowboys and Indians with a real 38 Colt pistol (the same one owned by my grandfather and eventually handed down to my grandson). I never loaded the pistol when I was playing, but I did target practice in my backyard many a time. Worse than playing cowboys and Indians, though, was that on occasion, I would carry the gun to school just for the heck of it. I never had any intention of shooting anyone. I just liked guns, and because my dad had taught me well, I was very safety conscious. I kept the gun well-hidden under my clothing, so I was never caught. I never threatened anyone. If I had been caught, I probably would have just been scolded and told never to do it again. Times change.

When the boys of the neighborhood got to be seven or eight years old, we began to paddle our bicycles to local swimming holes on French Creek, Two Mile Run, and a place about ten miles up and down hills called High Banks. I recall one time, several of the local boys and I were swimming at our Two-Mile Run swimming hole. One kid, Joe Neely, could not swim. The swimming hole was not deep, but there were spots well over our heads. The creek swept down between an old bridge slab and an eight- or ten-foot-high pillar still standing upright. The gap between the two was about ten feet. Joe wanted to get from the slab to the pillar over the gap but could not navigate the six- or seven- foot water flowing between the two. I overestimated my swimming ability a bit when I offered to carry Joe across on my back. We progressed not a foot across the gap with Joe clinging to my back. Joe had zero body fat. His deadweight pushed me underwater. I managed to walk on the bottom with Joe atop me to the other side. I never tried that again. On another occasion, I was swimming with my Boy Scout troop in a local swimming hole. I had not yet learned how to swim. I walked into the water and stepped in a hole. The water was over my head. One of the older boys dragged me out of the water. I really thought at the time I was going to drown. Thanks to the Boy Scouts and the YMCA, I did eventually learn how to swim. But to this day, I cannot say that I really enjoy swimming.

I recall another time that my good friend, Roy Shingledecker, and I were hiking in the forest which surrounded our small village. We came across an old tree that had two branches parallel to the ground. One was about five feet above a lower second branch. The second lower branch was about five feet away and about eight feet from the ground. The game we played was to leap from one limb to the other, grab the lower limb, then drop to the ground. I could make the jump quite easily. Roy was not so lucky. Three or four times, he made the leap catching the lower branch just by the tips of his fingers. He reached the lower limb just enough to swing his feet into the air. Down he would thump to the ground, back first with the wind knocked out of his lungs. When he sufficiently recovered, up he would climb and try the whole stunt over again. The incident was not funny for Roy, but as I write these words, I cannot stop myself from chuckling at the memory.

I remember another occasion when I and an acquaintance, John McCarthy, were walking home from Little League baseball practice. I no longer remember why, but I had had words with a Franklin boy. As we walked along a narrow tree and shrub path toward home, I heard the thundering of feet behind me. Coming at a fast pace toward me were the Franklin boy and his friends. I turned back to signal John. John was hightailing it out of there. I was left to confront the Franklin boy and his friends by myself. The Franklin boy and I quickly got into a brawl with all his friends standing in a tight circle around us. We were on the ground. I held onto the guy, quite afraid to punch my opponent. I thought for certain if I hurt the Franklin boy, he and his friends would pummel me into the dirt. We wrestled that way for a while. No damage to either of us resulted from our "all-out battle." Maybe the other guy was just as scared as I was and feared painful retaliation if he hurt me with a punch. The "fight" just petered out and we went on our separate ways.

To this day, I have not completely forgiven John for abandoning me. But I must admit that the event causes me to chuckle as I think about it. It is OK, John, I forgive you.

I informed my friend, Roy Shingledecker, of the incident. He and I walked to John's house and demanded John to go outside and explain his actions. His older brother, Tom, confronted Roy and me on their front porch. We were not going to get by Tom to his brother, who was crouching behind his screen door inside his house. Discretion being the greater part of valor, Roy and I left with our tails between our legs.

Another incident that still to this day does not seem to me to be all that funny occurred at a winter weekend Boy Scout camp out at Camp Coffman. I and other boys from our troop were returning from our hike when we were accosted by another troop of boys. The other boys began to pummel us with snowballs. I found myself on top of a little mound surrounded by the other boys. My troop of boys ran away to our cabin, which was just a short distance away, leaving me all alone. I fought furiously because I was very angry at my fellow troopers for abandoning me. Eventually, the other boys got tired of the one-sided snowball fight. To this day, I have not forgiven the bunch of cowards who abandoned me.

I did not always fight fair. There was a school fellow by the name of Gary. He and I did not get along. One day, Gary came past me in our crowded school hallway. As he passed by, he knocked my books out of my hand and continued on through the crowd of kids changing classes. I was furious and steamed all afternoon. Gary and I shared a tenth-grade homeroom. When I returned to the homeroom at the end of the day, Gary was already back in the room sitting in his aisle seat. I calmly walked back the aisle. When I reached his desk, without warning, I hit him hard with a sucker punch, knocking him out of his seat and onto the floor. I returned to my seat. About that time, the homeroom teacher entered the room and saw Gary rising from the floor. He asked what happened. Not a soul said a word. After that incident, Gary and I did not exactly get along, but he never confronted me again. Sadly, though, Gary died a few years ago. Long after the event, I continued to not like the guy. But I must say now, I regret not having the chance to meet him again and shake his hand.

School in those days was a bit different from now. Teachers had the legal right to whack you if you got out of line. The understanding among all the kids was that if one got a spanking at school, one could expect to get one when one got home. Few kids acted up much. I must say that I was a bit of an exception. I never got into any serious trouble in school, but I was a bit unruly at times. I was probably in about ninth or tenth grade when hurrying from one class to another, I descended a flight of stairs in several jumps. At the bottom of the stairs stood a teacher monitor. When I reached the bottom, he told me to go back up the stairs, then walk like a gentleman back down. When I reached the top of the stairs, I took off running. He chased me, but I managed to escape. I had a problem, though. He knew my class schedule, so he waited outside my classroom for me. I finally had to surrender. Off I was hauled to the principal's office. The principal was named Vern Alderson. He was a pretty good guy and knew me well. I remember him sitting me down in front of his desk and telling me that if I could ever get my act together, there was no telling how far I would go. He did not punish me, but asked me to apologize to the teacher. I did as he asked. I do not remember ever acting up in school again.

Growing up, I had a bit of a passion for blowing things up. I recall that I knew about an establishment that if one were tall enough to put one's money on the counter, they would sell you dynamite. So, when other kids were playing with firecrackers, I was tossing quarter sticks of dynamite about. My dad was quite tolerant about such shenanigans. But one day, neighbors complained that I was causing dishes to rattle off shelves, so my dad instructed me to stop throwing dynamite into the street in front of our house. I stopped, but I continued my dynamite antic in our nearby forest. One day, my friends and I dug some holes under a long string of huge rocks and placed dynamite sticks under them. We would light the fuse and run off some distance. When the dynamite went boom, chunks of rocks would rain down all about us. It is a wonder that none of us were seriously injured. We toppled more than one tree with dynamite. And dynamite made life miserable for many an anthill around our Christmas tree farm.

Early on, when I was too young for dynamite, I discovered that carbide and water make a great boom. I would place a small amount of carbide in an oil can and punch a small hole in the bottom. In the hole, I would stuff a cloth wick. My homemade bomb went off with a loud bang. The can would fly a hundred so feet in the air. Great fun.

When I was a teenager, our family had but one inexpensive record player and just a handful of vinyl records. I remember having one 45 rpm that I especially liked. When I was home alone, I often put on the one record I could call mine and danced to its music on our living room floor. I learned to become a smooth dancer with my own style. To this day, I can play in my mind two tunes on that record: *Young Love* and *Red Sails in the Sunset*. Many years later, I had the thrill of meeting Tab Hunter in person at his house in Santa Fe, New Mexico.

Because of those self-taught dancing lessons, I became a fairly good dancer. Sadly, in my late seventies, I lost most of my rhythm.

As I wrote about my mom's love of musicals, the thoughts of her brings to my mind the many musicals I learned to love. To this day, I can see clearly in my mind and hear Doris Day's lovely voice. I can play over and over in my mind Fred Astaire and Ginger Rogers dancing smoothly across their dance floor. I wish I would have taken my mom to a Broadway musical. She would have loved it.

After I graduated from Rocky Grove High School, I enrolled in Pennsylvania State University as a physics major. I continued my pole- vaulting career on Penn State's track team and got serious about boxing.

I spent hours in the on-campus boxing gym. I worked out regularly on a speed bag and heavy punching bag. When I would use the bags, I would always punch twice with my left hand to every punch with my right. I did countless one-arm push-ups, always two with my left arm to one with my right. I developed a very powerful left hook.

I recall one day when I seriously got my bell rung. I was sparing with a fellow and was working on a move that if done right could end a fight. The move involved dropping one's right hand to entice one's opponent to swing a right at one's head. The trick was to move one's head to the left just in time so that the punch flew past the right side of one's head. On this occasion, I mistimed the head movement. My opponent caught me square on my forehead with a very hard right. I saw stars as my knees buckled. Through sheer force of will, I righted myself. I was furious. The next thing I remember was the referee pulling me off the top of my opponent, who was flat on his back receiving a pummeling from me. That fight was the closest I ever came to going down for the county in a boxing match.

A year later, I transferred to Slippery Rock Teachers College where I started to informally box again. In the last fight, I remember, I and a tank of a guy were having it out in the basement of our dorm. The guy was getting the better of me. Finally, I backed him into a corner and punched him with everything left in me. My body looked like I had gotten in the ring with Rocky Balboa. The other guy looked a little worse. I never boxed again.

Back to my Penn State days. I am not proud to say that on not a few evenings, I would stroll around the campus looking for some suckers. When I found a couple of boys, I would mouth off to them. When they were about to take up fisticuffs, I would invite them to the boxing gym. The fights were never fair ones.

My time at Penn State was not all academic drudgery. Some of the escapes my friends and I pulled off are a bit embarrassing to relate. We lived on the fifth or sixth floor of an all-boys dorm. One evening, we scrounged some plywood and boarded up our rather large walk-in shower room. We sealed off the drains and filled the shower room with about three feet of water. It is a wonder that the floor did not collapse with all the weight. After swimming about for an hour or so, we unplugged all the drains. Whoosh! The water rushed down to the lower floors. In the morning, we heard many stories of guys getting their butts well-hosed off while sitting on the can.

In another incident, us boys would stand on our fifth or sixth floor hallway overlooking a window above a pass-through under the building. When girls would walk by, we would drop water-filled balloons on their heads. A great laugh for us, but not so funny for the girls.

We noticed that there was a long line of metal garbage cans down both sides of a long mall leading to one of the main buildings. The cans were lined with burlap bags. One night, we removed the can lids and dropped fire into every can. What a blazing sight that was. Lucky for us, we never got caught.

All throughout school grounds were underground tunnels, which carried steam heat to each building. All the tunnels had outlets into campus buildings. Had we ever discovered an outlet to the girls' dormitories, our sense of being gentlemen would have been sorely tested. A few of us guys spent many an evening exploring those tunnels. Often, we would burst out in a building much to startled folks standing along our escape route. Lucky for us, we were never caught.

I recall a life-changing time at Penn State. I felt myself struggling with college course material. All my years of priding myself in never taking a lesson home in grade school and high school were coming back to haunt me. I had just finished my first test and was certain that I had failed. I remember sitting at my tiny desk in my dorm room staring at the wall and crying inside. How could I ever tell my mom and dad that I was a failure? I spent two hours staring in silence at that wall. Finally, I got myself out of the funk. I told myself that never again would I punish myself that way. I told myself that in the future, I would ask only one question: "Did I do the best I knew how?" And if I could answer that question "yes," the hell with it and what anyone else might think. I never punished myself that way again for the rest of my life in spite of many failures.

Penn State was 132 miles from my home. I had very little money, so the only way to get home on weekends was to hitchhike. Unfortunately for me, in their wisdom, Penn State scheduled Saturday classes. Mine was chemistry lab. I cut the class many times, which surely contributed to the "D" grade I was awarded for my lack of effort. On many weekends, I hitchhiked home. I remember one occasion when two businessmen stopped to give me a ride. Along the way, they stopped for dinner and invited me to join them. I demurred. They asked me if the problem was that I had no money. I had to admit that was true. They invited me to dine with them and paid the bill. I wish I would have remembered their names so that I could have thanked them in later years. I recall another time when I was on my way back to Penn State. The night became rather cold and snow started to fall. Many cars passed me in the night. As each would pass without stopping, I would fire a snowball at the back of their car. I made the mistake of bouncing a snowball off of an unmarked State trooper car. The troopers screeched to a halt. One policeman got out of the car to confront me. When he discovered that I was a Penn State student hitchhiking back to school, he told me to behave myself and drove off, leaving me shivering in the wind. At that point, I would have preferred to be arrested. At least I would have been able to escape the cold. I did not make it back to Penn State until quite late that night.

After the end of one year at Penn State, I transferred to Slippery Rock State Teachers College in Slippery Rock, Pennsylvania. The "Rock" was only thirty miles from my mom and dad's home. Hitchhiking home was no big deal and Slippery Rock cost only $850 a year. I was able to pay much of my college costs by working in the summers and having a part-time job as a short-order cook during my last two years of school. Years before, my Grandpa Cole gave to my father the old Heasley farm of about 150 acres. On that farm, my dad planted Christmas trees. For many summers, I mowed the grass between those trees, trimmed them, and cut and bundled them for sale. I was never paid a salary for the work, but had the understanding that profits from the sale of Christmas trees would help with my college costs. My sister, Darlene, also worked on the farm when she got older, but was a little cleverer than I was. She negotiated a small hourly salary for herself and a few of her friends.

My life changed quite dramatically when at Slippery Rock I met Mary Carol Vensel, who was a freshman. She was a very diligent student and encouraged me to be the same. Neither of us had any extra money to spend. I recall going to the student union with Carol and sharing one coke. Regular Saturday night dances were free, so we often spent Saturday nights dancing. Mostly because I was tired of being poor, I graduated from the Rock just three and a half years after starting college at Penn State. In those times, colleges permitted one to take courses by final exam. I was able to pick up a few math courses that way. In one semester, I racked up twenty-seven credit hours. I never earned less than eighteen credit hours.

When I graduated from Slippery Rock in January 1961, I was lucky enough to find a job teaching ninth grade students for one semester in a small new state town called Addison not far from Corning, New York. Teaching was great fun and I fully intended to return to the profession, but I decided that I needed more world experience to be a really good teacher. The course I taught was geographic and history of the United States. The course had no fixed lesson outline, so I was able to teach pretty much what I wanted. I remember one class session at which I put on a one-person play about the beginning of World War II. I played the part of the several key characters in that drama. Leading the Germans in the attack on Poland was a German general by the name of Gudarian. As I related the early morning of the attack, I lowered and lowered the voice of Gudarian. The kids by this time were sitting on the edge of their seats. At the moment of Gudarian's command to attack, I struck my desk with a swagger stick. The children jumped out of their seats.

I recall another time when I was doing student teaching at Moniteau High School, I was assigned a class of senior misfits, most of whom could not read or write very well. As an alternative to a written test, I offered the students the option to draw a picture of an American history event. One kid drew a picture of the Hamilton-Burr duel. In the picture, the kid depicted Burr with a large bore pistol with a large bullet screaming out of his pistol toward Hamilton. For Hamilton, he pictured a small pistol with a bullet dribbling out of his gun. Over Hamilton was a caption, "Oh shit." I gave the kid an "A." Another kid depicted a scene from a naval battle of the Barbary Wars. In the scene was a soldier coming down in a parachute. Above that soldier was a caption "What the hell am I doing here. I gave the kid an A.

In August, I enlisted in the United States Air Force. Complements of the USAF, I boarded my first jet plane flight from Pittsburgh to San Antonio, Texas, to begin Officers Training School at Lackland AFB. Mostly, what I remember of that flight was landing in San Antonio, Texas. When I stepped off the plane, I was shocked by the hottest temperatures I had ever experienced in my life and what seemed to me a gigantic sky. As usual, I had no money because, except for a small amount needed for laundry and haircuts, I sent all my pay home to Carol. One evening, late in our training cycle, I was sitting by myself in the barracks dayroom feeling sorry for myself. All the other cadets were at a small cadet officer's club enjoying themselves on the one and only time during our training when "management" did not find some cadet infraction which caused the club to be closed. An older, prior service, Mustang cadet happened by. When I related to him why I was not going to the club, he handed me five dollars. I paid him back before we graduated. I have never forgotten his kindness.

I guess because I had no money to fool around and because I was driven to succeed, I graduated in the top five percent of my class and thus was awarded a "regular" commission. Everyone else received a reserve officer commission. This was a big deal and served me well when I was given my first operational assignment. Training in the intense heat at Lackland AFB was often grueling. We were given a white towel to place on the very hot, white pebble-covered parade grounds to perform our PT routines. Without the tile, the white pebbles would have blistered our hands. Often as the whole 750 student body stood at attention on a boiling hot parade ground, a few cadets would pass out and fall to the ground. Finally, a cadet died from heat exhaustion. After that incident, the air force changed the rules. When the heat index (temperature and humidity) got above a certain level, parade ground activities were suspended.

I quickly learned that giving 110 percent effort 100 percent of the time was not possible. So, I picked and chose the times when I would put out the maximum. I recall a one-mile training run we were ordered to perform. At the end of the run, I sprinted the last hundred yards or so where a training officer stood observing our efforts. When I finished the run, I staggered over to a chain-link fence and vomited. The training officer never forgot me.

A month or so after graduation from Officer Training School, I was sent to Biloxi, Mississippi, for forty-three weeks of communications electronics training. I really struggled in that course. I knew nothing about electricity or electronics. Almost all my classmates were electrical engineer graduates. When we got to the radar block, my electrical engineer classmates and I were on a level playing field. They knew nothing about radar either. I got the highest grade on that block. How sweet it was.

After graduation and commissioning, I was assigned to Eighth Air Force located at Westover AFB, Massachusetts, as OIC of a ground-to-air radio site. As a second lieutenant, I was really green. On my first day, I gathered the leading NCOs together and gave them a little speech. I told them that I knew nothing about what they did and so it would depend entirely upon them. I told them that I ask only one thing. I ask them to always tell me the truth. In return, I promised to do all in my power to take care of their needs. Early on, I was afforded the opportunity to hold up my end of the bargain. For the senior NCOIC, I was required to write an efficiency report. I gave the NCOIC high marks. When my boss, a full colonel, reviewed my rating, he ordered me to lower my scores. I refused and informed the colonel that I could not in good conscience do as he ordered. I told him that it was his choice to write something different in his endorsement, but not to demand that I change my rating. The rating went through as I had written it. Word was not long getting back to my troops.

I recall another incident when one of my radio operators got a local girl pregnant. Off I hauled him to the Catholic girl's home to explain himself to the nuns. For some reason, the boy and the girl did not want to get married. So, as a compromise, the boy agreed to pay for the girl's pregnancy. That was the end of it.

I recall another incident that haunts me to this day. The time was early in the Vietnam War. In those days, most who went to Vietnam were volunteers. The policy changed to direct assignments, but with the caveat that a named assignee could escape assignment to Vietnam if a fellow airman could go in one's place. One from my unit did. He was killed shortly after arriving in Vietnam.

Shortly after being assigned as OIC of a ground-to-air radio site at Westover, I wangled my way into a computer programming school. I learned that a qualifying test was required. I went to the testing location to take the test. The instructor told me I was not on his list. I told him, "Damn if I know, my commander told me to take the test", a little stretch of the truth. He permitted me to take the test and I qualified. Then, I discovered the name of the officer who was assigned the additional duty of slotting candidates for computer classes. I bugged him every week. Just to get rid of me, he gave me a programming school assignment. I knew not a thing about computer programming and not the foggiest what a "computer program" was. All I knew was that the civilian programmers who worked at our base made a lot of money. The air force sent me back to Biloxi, Mississippi, for a sixteen-week programming school. The first few days in class were a mystery to me. The instructor kept talking about a thing called "computer program." I kept wracking my brain but could only come up with a blank. After a few days, a light came on in my head and I was off and running toward a career as a computer programmer.

Before I got the bright idea of becoming a computer programmer, I got another bright idea. Many days, I wandered off base to the Eighth Air Force underground command post. There, I discovered

Ned M Cole, Jr.

ITT computer programmers, but also ground-based Strategic Air Command Airborne Command and Control officers. They got flight pay of about two hundred dollars a month. That was the job for me. So, I scheduled myself for an altitude training test and spent as much time with the air controllers as I could manage. I used my standard line, "Damn if I know, my commander told me to take the test," to be admitted to the test session. When I thought that I was sufficiently prepared, I went to our squadron commander and petitioned him to recommend me for Airborne Control school. He agreed. But not soon after, I discovered ITT highly paid computer programmers, so again, I petitioned our commander. He was a bit disappointed in me, but agreed to release me if I could get a programming school slot assignment. He was thinking short term. I was thinking long term. I had no plans to make the air force a career. The defining moment in my choice of plans for the future was one day when I and a number of other young officers attended a "retention" briefing." I guess the briefer thought that he was talking to a room full of pilots and navigators. In any event, he informed us that flying officers had great career potential. Not so much for ground pounders like me.

Not long after programming school, I found myself stationed at HQ SAC, Offutt AFB, Omaha, Nebraska, working on the Strategic Air Command's Command Control System. There, Carol and I met David and Joanne McQueston. We have remained friends ever since.

In June 1967, I resigned my commission and entered the civilian labor force. My first job was with Auerbach Corporation, a consulting firm located in downtown Philadelphia. I accepted the job for one reason: it paid the most. My salary for a year was twelve thousand five hundred dollars. I remember talking to a civilian friend I knew when on active duty about our future earning potential. I remember us agreeing that if we could ever earn a kilo buck (one thousand dollars) a month and own a twenty-thousand-dollar house, we would indeed be in high cotton. I figured that my next job would be a percentage higher than my salary at Auerbach. I remember a

Jewish colleague at Auerbach telling me that one was worth whatever one was willing to pay one.

About eighteen months later, I found a job at Union Switch and Signal ("The Switch") located in Swissvale, Pennsylvania, a suburb of Pittsburgh. I was finally back home.

After a year or so as a civilian, our family had a need to send our deaf son, Jon, to a special school. The problem was that the school cost two hundred or three hundred dollars a month, which we did not have. I happened to spot an ad in our local paper for an Air National Guard communications officer. The job just happened to pay about two hundred fifty dollars a month, so I became a weekend ANG warrior. I stayed with the Pennsylvania Air National Guard for about eleven years as commander of a small communications unit. When I arrived, the unit had not in recent years deployed for annual two weeks of training. I changed that. Soon, the unit started to deploy in alternate years to Patrick AFB, Florida, and Norton AFB, California. We were lucky that our Pittsburgh base was home to a tanker wing, so transportation was not an issue. For 1980, I scheduled our annual training to take place at Norton AFB. Norton is just outside Pasadena, California, where the 1980 Super Bowl was to be played. Luck would have it, the Steelers made it to the Super Bowl. A secretary at the Switch was dating a Steeler. Through her Steeler friend, tickets were arranged for all of my unit, plus a few extra tickets. The Air Wing got us to Norton, and locals at Norton got us to the Super Bowl. A couple of months later, I transferred to the New York Air National Guard. I guess it must have been tough for the next commander to top my game.

Not long after I transferred to the New York Air Guard, the unit got a new commander. His name was Jack Ianozzie. Colonel Ianozzie was the best commander I ever had. When he took over the unit, the unit was a mess. In short order, he changed the unit into a first-class organization. When I first arrived, Ianozzie was not the commander. I was an outsider, so I was stuck back in a corner. At an exercise at Fort Drum, I was assigned to an out-of- the-way spot where the unit commander assumed I could do no harm. With me in the small group of "liaison" folks were three lieutenant colonels, one from each service. I was a major. I had a great deal of experience preparing and giving presentations, so I prepared a set of colorful flip charts which depicted the whole exercise. Word got around that if a dignitary wanted to understand what was going on, one should stop by our office. At the end of the exercise, the three lieutenant colonels put me in for the New York Commendation Medal. Luck would have it, the very first drill at which Colonel Ianozzie took command, the medal arrived. The good colonel pinned the decoration onto my uniform. After that, I could do no wrong. Later on, I came up with a new plan for our annual training exercises. Our unit was group headquarters for some fifteen or so radar control units around the country. For our annual two-week training at Otis AFB, Massachusetts, I set up an advance team which by radio guided all the incoming units to their assigned site. My understanding is that Tactical Air Command picked up the idea and ran with it.

I regularly flew from my home in Chicago to Syracuse, New York to attend monthly weekend drills. On one occasion, I happened to be working in Datong, China, when a drill weekend was scheduled for a few days, hence, I hopped on an airplane, and about thirty hours and 8,485 miles later, I arrived Friday evening in Syracuse. As far as I know, I hold the world record for distance commuted to an ANG weekend drill.

When I was on active duty, my time away from home was very difficult for me. I was very homesick. I remember my time in Biloxi, Mississippi, sitting at my small desk writing a letter to my dad. I am embarrassed to admit that I cried as I wrote the letter. I do not recall that I even told Carol how homesick I was. Sometime along the line, I got over being homesick. Now, wherever I live feels like home.

Back to my time at Union Switch and Signal. I clearly remember standing on the front portico of the Switch when Roy Mapes, soon to be my boss, offered me a job for fourteen thousand five hundred dollars as a computer programmer. Years later, Roy told me that hiring me was one of the best decisions he ever made. He told me that he had to pay me more money than he made to bring me aboard. Roy told me that the next day, his boss called him into his office and informed him that the salary I was offered would not do. He immediately offered Roy a raise.

A month or two after I joined the Switch in November 1968, I was soon promoted to supervisor of the Canadian Pacific Railroad Alyth Railroad Yard computerization project. The only significant difference I discovered was the change from an hourly employee to a supervisor meant that I worked longer hours, but did not get paid overtime.

My time at the Switch was one of the most fun times I had working. Often on Sunday evenings, I would become quite antsy. I could not wait to return to work Monday morning.

I was assigned the job of supervising the Alyth Yard computer control project system design, programming, and coding. Working with me to complete the project was a group of eight or ten computer programmers. The project was more than a bit daunting. The man-hours and time to complete estimates were made before I arrived. I quickly determined that the project cost would double, and the completion date would extend for a year or so longer than first anticipated. I caught a considerable amount of flack when I announced my findings. Our team completed the project inside my estimate of time and money. Early in the project, I prepared what came to be known as our "Do Book." I went through the entire customer specification and prepared detailed specifications for all the computer programs it would take to implement the system. Our Do Book became very popular with our customer, the Canadian Pacific Railroad, and became a standard for all future railroad hump yard projects. The project was the most sophisticated system of its day. Much of what we designed had never been designed before. The project was more than a bit daunting. The man-hours and time to complete estimates were made before I arrived. I quickly determined that the project cost would double, and the completion date would extend for a year or so longer than first anticipated. I caught a considerable amount of flack when I announced my findings. Our team completed the project inside my estimate of time and money. Early in the project, I prepared what came to be known as our "Do Book." I went through the entire customer specification and prepared detailed specifications for all the computer programs it would take to implement the system. Our Do Book became very popular with our customer, the Canadian Pacific Railroad, and became a standard for all future railroad hump yard projects. The project was the most sophisticated system of its day. Much of what we designed had never been designed before.

As was the Switch's standard process, billings were paramount. Shipment meant billings. So, long before we were finished with all programming efforts, our computers were shipped to Calgary. As a result, much of our time completing the project was spent on-site in Canada.

Our computer for the project was a Honeywell 516. The computer had thirty-two thousand 16-bit words of memory and a two hundred fifty thousand 16-bit word disk. The computer operated at one million cycles per second. Today's computers have millions of bytes of memory and operate thousands of times faster. Today, a small flash memory has billions of bytes of memory. Computers in the 1960s came with assembly software to convert coding to object form and an object loader to convert object to digital. The computers came with blank memory except for a few boot instructions and no device driver software. We had to code all the software drivers ourselves. How we were able to make the computers work so wonderfully with so little to work with, to this day, still astounds me.

One of the critical programming tasks was to write disk driver software. The young gentleman I assigned to this task was a complete failure. I only discovered his failure a few days after arriving in Calgary. I fired the gentleman and remembered a very solemn late evening when I sat by my lonesome studying the flowchart of the disk driver software the gentleman had been working on. I remember slowly folding up the flowcharts and dropping them in a waste basket. With a clean piece of paper, I started again. In a few long days, I completed the task and we were off and running. Unfortunately, I created a bug in the driver software that bugged us for months. Once a month or so, the computer would crash. A digital dump of memory yielded only garbage. One late evening in Calgary, I sat silently in front of the computer thinking about the problem. Eureka! I remembered the disk driver software I had written earlier and I remembered that I had forgotten to shut off computer interrupts when inside the disk driver subroutine. What happened was on returning to the subroutine after the interrupt, the computer lost the subroutine return address. Off the program flew into memory crashing and banging its way to a crash. A couple of digital patches to the program cured the problem. Only years later could I muster the courage to admit to anyone that I had been the cause of the computer crashes. The work in Calgary was great fun. Several of my team I left in Swissvale to complete coding tasks for programs designed by myself and other members of our team. At the time, I came up with a rather unique way of conveying my designs to my coders. At that time, as was standard practice, one started the design process by creating a flowchart. But I came up with a method designed so that I could commit the desired logic to line-by-line written words. The idea was unique enough to get published in a widely- circulated computer nerd magazine called *Datamation*.

Our time in Canada was mostly spent checking out the programs coded by others. I loved checking out coding. A great programmer assigned to our team was a fellow named Bill Watso, who created a clever piece of software that permitted one to advance step by step through a program to check out coding. I followed the one line of code method with a religious fever. Consequently, I was able to check out hundreds of programs resulting in zero bugs (with the disk driver exception).

Hard as I tried, I could not convince the rest of my checkout team to follow my method. All of them, except Bill Watso, were of the let-her-rip-and-fix- what-errors-came-up-later mentality.

Bill Watso was one of the best coders I ever knew. I could not beg Bill to create flowcharts before coding. He just coded straight out of his head with zero errors. Bill saved me from crashing and burning on that project. I knew nothing about mass storage data manipulation. Bill wrote software for us that was every bit as sophisticated as Bill Gates's DOS system. Bill Watso was a lot of things, but not a sober one. On regular occasions, he would disappear for a day or two to go on an alcoholic bender. One day, when we were nearing the end of the project, Bill was working back in Swissvale. As was his custom, Bill worked late at night. Bill was not an especially sociable guy. One night, he became enraged by overflowing waste baskets. He carried all the baskets to the vice president of engineering's office and emptied them. The next day, Bill was fired. I did not learn of the firing until I returned a few weeks later to Swissvale. It was too late to save Bill. Thank you, Bill, for saving me. If only I could have returned the favor. I loved that guy.

One outcome of Bill getting fired was that my boss ordered me to complete flowcharts of Bill's coding that Bill would never complete. I spent many days of drudgery studying Bill's assembly language programs and did my best to reverse-engineer flowcharts. I must admit that I often got lost in Bill's very complicated coding. The result was a series of flowcharts that did not accurately represent Bill's elegant design. I pity the poor programmer who tried to use those flowcharts to recreate Bill's software.

After the Alyth job, I was assigned to manage an upgrade project for a railroad located in Kansas City, Kansas, and another upgrade for the Union Pacific Railroad in the small town of North

Platte, Nebraska. Both jobs were largely uneventful except for an incident with the lone programmer assigned to the North Platt job. He was an alcoholic. One night, he was stopped and arrested for DUI. I had to fly to North Platte to bail him out and testify at his hearing. I explained to the judge that the man needed his car to get to work. The judge settled for a fine and forbade the guy to use his car for anything but to get to work. The guy did not stop drinking but avoided another DUI.

A few weeks after I arrived at the Switch, a funny incident to me occurred on the original installation of the Kansas City hump yard control system. The Switch had a bunch of us computer nerds on-site to try to get the system up and running. I was assigned to the team, but knew not a thing about the system.

So, I was assigned the low-level task of writing code for an IBM printing machine. IBM gave us no instructions for the machine, so I had to one by one send codes to the machine to determine which codes caused the machine to do what. After a few days, I got the machine working. Since the machine spit out something that seemed real, the Kansas City RR chief engineer became convinced that I was the only one that knew what I was doing. He demanded that the Switch keep me on-site. I had a great time for two weeks. My only job was to show up each day.

During my eleven years at the Switch, I was tapped to give many presentations at railroad conventions. I guess no one else in the company volunteered. Giving those presentations were a lot of fun. I only had to speak for about twenty minutes and then had the rest of the convention to have fun. Because of my presentation skills, I got tapped as the go-to guy to make presentations to our sales team at their twice-yearly sales meetings. It was great for me. Every winter, I got to accompany the salesmen to their Florida meetings. A one-hour presentation, then the rest of the week was party time and golf for me. I was not the most popular engineer, but the sales guys held me in high regard.

In the mid-1970s, I was "promoted" to marketing product manager with a staff of zero. The job was not much fun. My mentor, Glenn Stinson, sent me to the University of Pittsburgh for my MBA while retaining my full-time job at the Switch and commander of an ANG unit. A tough two years of little sleep and no play followed. I was joined at my MBA program by Lou Kopsa. Lou pointed out to me that I was entitled to GI Bill assistance. So, I contacted a GI Bill administrator. Sure enough, I was eligible. The administrator told me that it didn't matter that my company was picking up the whole tab. For the two years I was in the MBA program, I collected, tax-free, eight hundred fifty dollars a month. Nice! One just got to love the government.

Lou was the head of HR at the Switch. Lou and I had many interactions at the time and more than a few arguments. I remember Lou once saying to me, "Ned, you may not always be right, but you are never in doubt." I suspect there is a bit of truth in Lou's claim. My oldest daughter, Carrie, and my second daughter, Regina, most likely inherited an identical gene from me.

More than once, people expressed the opinion that I was a bit bullheaded. Such was true if I thought I was right. But my saving grace was that if facts proved me wrong, on many occasions I did a complete 180 change of mind. Folk who worked for me and knew me well understood that I could be highly certain about a course of action, but presented with facts would change course on a dime. I never had a problem admitting when I was proven to be wrong.

A couple of years later, I was moved to our strategic planning department to work on our five-year strategic plans.

After a couple of years in purgatory, I was transferred back to engineering to manage the Baltimore Rapid Transit project. That job was a blast. As soon as I was assigned the job, our team was given a large open-floor space for our offices. We hauled from storage a few old desks and chairs. I set up my desk right in the middle of the room, placed a small American flag on my desk, and announced that "this is headquarters." I instructed my team to put a sign at the entrance to our open space: "You are about to enter the finest engineering team in the world, The Tiger Team." I spent a very fun year and a half running that project. Near the end of the project, I was transferred to headquarters American Standard on 40 West Fortieth Street, New York, New York. I managed to convince one of the lead engineers on the Baltimore city consulting team to take over the project when I left. While running the Baltimore project, I was assigned the task of writing our response to Miami's specifications for a control system which was nearly identical to the Baltimore transit system specifications. Traditionally, the practice was to fill several boxes of boiler plate and deliver that along with our dollar bid to the customer. We often spend one hundred thousand dollars or so preparing such a tomb. I decided to just write a fifty-page submittal specifically addressing each line of the customer's RFQ. I was convinced that that is all the customer wanted. Glenn trusted my judgment. We won the twenty-seven-million-dollar project bid by just a few hundred thousand.

I recall one time a few months into the Baltimore project, we ran into a snag. Baltimore engineers made a mistake in their specifications. The GE electric "chopper" locomotives output a nasty signal that interfered with the signaling system. I spoke to our engineers. They told me for twenty-five thousand dollars, they could design a filter that solved the problem. Modifying the locomotives was a nonstarter, so off I went one afternoon to Baltimore to negotiate a change order. I started out by telling the Baltimore people that the change would cost five hundred thousand dollars because of all the documentation the government would require. We argued late into the night. Finally, one of the Baltimore engineers, who was an ex-air force officer, invited me to his room. I guess Baltimore hoped that somehow this guy could appeal to my better half. We finally agreed to two hundred fifty thousand dollars provided the only documentation we had to provide were handwritten engineering notes. When I got back to the Switch, the vice president of sales, Bob Fisher, stomped into my office and demanded that I tell him what I did. He told me, "Ned, you know that the Switch absolutely does not accept any markup of less than 30 percent." I told him about the twenty-five-thousand-dollars engineering estimate and the two hundred fifty thousand dollars Baltimore agreed to. He turned and left my office without another word. I never heard another peep by management about the subject. My guess is that when Fisher got back to his office and told the GM the story, they had a good laugh. I am not especially proud of this incident, but my job was to maximize company profits, so I justified to myself my actions.

While I was still working as a strategic planner at the Switch, I was asked to come off my two-week ANG training in California to give a presentation to the L&N Railroad for a five-site computerized central traffic control system. I avoided being AWOL by leaving California after midnight and returning before the next midnight. My troops covered for me. At the end of my presentation, the railroad's chief engineer announced, "That is exactly what I have been looking for." The chief engineer was the one guy who was not always a Switch friend. Our vice president of sales, Bob Fisher, said to the chief engineer, "I will pass your recommendation on to your VPO." We then proceeded to a meeting with the VPO. The VPO asked Bob Fisher, "How are we going to do this?" Bob answered, "Just send a telegram to GRS that you have decided to award a sole order contract to the Switch."

The L&N VPO agreed. We were awarded a multimillion-dollar, multisite contract. I can tell you that by the time I deplaned from my first-class flight back to California I was a bit inebriated. Lucky for me, my second in command, Bill Seine, gathered me up and hauled me back to our barracks just in time to beat my midnight deadline.

The leader of our planning section while I was still at the Switch was Paul Dunn. Paul was a brilliant guy, a very talented staff analyst, but was not cut out for leadership. After being assigned to "manage" our strategic planning department, Paul was assigned to be vice president of engineering and, again, my direct boss. In about 1983, Glenn brought Paul to work for us at Railroad Products Group headquartered in Chicago. Glenn Stinson asked me what I thought of Paul before offering him a job. I told Glenn straight out my misgiving about Paul as a leader. Our disagreement about Paul's qualifications was just one of the many differences of opinion between Glenn and me. As things turned out, Paul became a great staff analyst asset to our company. Glenn never put Paul in a leadership position. Earl Calendar, another Switch colleague, was assigned to the same planning section as was I, Earl was moved from the head of Switch's research and development engineering section. His brother was my first sergeant at the 172nd Communications Flight, PAANG. One of my old computer programming friends took over research and development engineering. He set the Switch on a path away from relays toward solid state technology.

My strategic planning job at 40 West Fortieth Street just across from Bryant Park was not much fun, but I got to hobnob around the world in the company's private jet rubbing elbows with company bigwigs. That part was fun. After two years, the planning department at American Standard was mostly disbanded. The near complete disbanding was largely due to a conversation I had with Keith Bunnel, a senior vice president of the company. Keith asked me what I thought of strategic planning of the sort we did. I gave him a truthful report of what a terrible waste of time the whole effort was. I told him that what happened to each yearly five-year plan developed by the company's divisions at great expense was that the plan was thrown in a drawer and not looked at again until the next year. I think to this day that the way strategic planning was conducted at that time by most companies in the United States was a gigantic waste of time.

Lucky for me, just before strategic planning at American Standard was essentially shut down, my old mentor from my Union

Switch and Signal days, Glenn Stinson, recruited me to join Railroad Products Group, Abex Corporation, a subsidiary of IC Industries Corporation. The great thing about the move was I got a big raise and was made vice president of marketing. The VP marketing position was a made-up job. Glenn brought me on to reorganize the company for two years, hence when he took over as president. From May 1982 until June of 1986, I had a great time. I took on the task of building a modern company-wide computer system from the ground up. While playing at being the ones and zeroes guy, Glenn also assigned me to manage several plant closedowns and several equipment installation projects. One of the disappointments I had was not being appointed general manager of our Trackwork division. I was Glenn's choice, but he was overruled by corporate management. The job went to a very talented outside guy named Ray Jean. Ray and I became good friends. I never held his selection for division general manager against him. He won the job fair and square. He turned out to be a great general manager, moved on to much higher positions in other companies, and amassed a considerable fortune. I recall what really was a job interview with the Abex president turned out to cost me the promotion. I was invited to fly on a company jet from New Jersey to Chicago with the president and several other company executives. I foolishly took a seat a few rows away from the president rather than sit in the seat facing him. More naively, I wore a cheap light blue suit. All the other executives aboard the aircraft wore one-thousand-dollar dark pinstripe suits. I guess my Scotsman heritage discouraged me from spending funds needed by my family on such frivolous items as clothing. Perhaps, it was my "shanty Irish" heritage inherited from my Irish grandfather, Harry Murrin. No doubt my mother is looking down from heaven with a scowl on her face for her son harboring such blasphemous thoughts. Either way, my lack of understanding of corporate culture most likely cost me a promotion to general manager of the Trackwork division.

In 1986, President Glenn Stinson, Vice President Jim Hinel, and I engineered a leveraged buyout of RPG from IC Industries. Although I continued with my fun ones and zeroes job, my relationship with Glenn turned very sour. At the closing for us buying the company, I knew that something was seriously wrong. I later learned that my problems with Glenn originated with a gentleman by the name of Michael Bayles. Michael was a subordinate of mine brought in and assigned to me by Glenn. I took Michael under my wing and promoted his advancement at Union Switch and later at Abex Corporation. I considered him a friend. However, Glenn told me that Michael had told him some things about me just before closing on our buyout deal that were very disturbing to Glenn. Most likely, Michael told Glenn about my many tantrums about Glenn's often destructive actions. I often confided in Michael. Michael was a good friend of Glenn's sons and often spent a good deal of time at Glenn's house. Glenn promised to tell me what Michael said, but never did. Being stabbed in the back by a guy I considered a friend is painful. In the last day I spoke to Michael, I told him that I had always considered him a friend, and for that reason, I would never do anything to hurt him, but I also would never again do anything to help him. I do not know if Michael is dead or alive today.

I remember excusing myself from the buyout closing session at the bank offices and going to the restroom to vomit. I walked back to our offices myself. Later that day, I wrote a note to myself which I still have. In essence, the note was to remind me that the hell I was about to live through was worth the payoff at the end. Hell, it was for the next three years. Was it all worth it? You betcha. I must add, though, without my long-time mentor, Glenn Stinson, the cooperation of IC Industries leadership, the First National Bank of Chicago, and too many others to list, the buyout would have never happened. Glenn banished me to a small office in the back of our building. I had a great deal of fun managing my small group of computer programmers, but a miserable time in my relationship with Glenn.

About three years later, Glenn retired when we sold a majority interest in our company to venture capitalist, Kolberg and Company. Two weeks before Glenn was to retire, Glenn called me into his office and told me to clean out my desk by the end of the day. He told me, "And you know why." I said to him, "Glenn, I am sorry things turned out this way." I guess Glenn fired me because he got tired of me telling the truth about what I thought about some of his actions. I turned away and quietly walked out of his office. Company personnel went into shock. The final closing for the sale actually stretched on for six weeks. Many years later, Glenn sent me a nice note when he learned of my son Jon's death. In spite of our estrangement, I always sent Glenn a copy of Carol's Christmas letter. In her 1999 letter, Carol told the story of our son Jonathan's death in 1998. The response to that Christmas letter was a very kind note from Glenn. That note was the only communication I ever received from Glenn after he fired me. That note was the closest we ever came to a reconciliation. Glenn died in 2017. I truly loved Glenn Stinson, but I also hated the terrible way he often treated people. There were times that Glenn could have gotten me to walk right through the gates of hell. There were other times that I could barely restrain myself from giving him a good belt on the nose. Oftentimes, I went back to my office and cursed to myself for half an hour after one of what seemed to me to be an unforgiveable outburst by Glenn. I vividly recall an incident when Glenn called me into his office to witness a telephone call; he wanted me to witness his conversation. Glenn liked having an audience when he was about to do something nasty. He called our Pueblo Trackwork plant to inform them that they had to fire one clerk. He told the manager that he would wait on the line until the manager gave him a name. Just after he ended the telephone call, he called one of our accounting ladies into his office and demanded some information from her. She shook like a leaf and stumbled through an explanation about what Glenn was asking. He threw her out of his office. He told me he was tired of people shaking when they came into his office. I told him, "Glenn, they shake because they are afraid of you." He said to me, "I will fire anyone who is afraid of me."

But after having been fired by Glenn, I again dodged a bullet. The incoming president, Don Grinter, hired me back with back pay to the date of firing and gave me Glenn's desk. I was finally back in a lakefront office. Don told me he had a good laugh on Glenn later when he told Glenn that not only had he hired me back, but he had also given me Glenn's desk and an office right next to his (the president's) office. And to make it sweeter, my good friend, VP human resources, Dick Spencer, arranged to see that I got two-week severance pay and several weeks of unused vacation pay. Actually, no one ever kept track of vacation days taken off by executives. Dick just arbitrarily decided I was owned three or four weeks. In Illinois, one was employed entirely at the whim of one's manager. There was not a thing I could do about being fired. I did learn that a few weeks before Glenn departed, he gave sizable bonuses to all high-ranking personnel. I had accomplished a great deal the past year and had saved the company a great deal of money. So, I wrote a letter to Glenn detailing about what I had accomplished for the company and advised him that I thought I was entitled to a bonus. To my surprise, I received a check for twenty-five thousand dollars in the mail a few days later. I swear I was born with a silver bullet gene.

In 1992, I retired at age fifty-two from ABC Rail Corporation, and not long after, I sold all of my stock in the company. Shortly after retirement, I was hired as a consultant to assist in negotiating a joint venture contract with the People's Republic of China. Later, I became the general manager and project manager of an effort to build a cast steel railroad plant in Datong, China. The experience in Datong was a blast, but the nearly two years of seven-day weeks and long-hour days nearly killed me. I came home in late 1997 after long several days in a Chinese hospital. The project was almost finished. Not long after, I had open-heart bypass surgery.

The Chinese hospital I was in was very old, pealing ceilings, dirty wall paint, and a bathroom that was very dirty and filled with junk. Naked light bulbs hung from the ceiling. Each day, an old lady with a dirty bucket of gray water came into my room and swabbed the floor. All she accomplished was to spread the dirt around. The only useable bathroom was a very dirty communal bathroom down the hall with a long trough with dripping water for a urinal. The bed in my room was a low cot with a thin hard mattress.

Next to my cot was another cot where the Chinese placed a minder twenty- four-seven. He was not a minder. The Chinese wanted to make certain that someone was watching over me day and night. They really tried to do their best to take care of me. The first day, a Chinese nurse gave me an antibiotic shot with a long needle. In two or three days, I felt better enough to insist that I be discharged from the hospital.

When I was first sent to Datong to become the general manager of Datong ABC Wheel Casting Company and the de facto project manager, I was sent all alone. In a few months of the projects, the American company sent Larry DeBoer, a very good, retired cast steel engineer, to help. I turned over all the engineering supervision to Larry. Larry saved my butt. Working with me were about thirty Chinese engineers and two wonderful interpreters. One was assigned as my assistant. I maintain email contact with my assistant, Larry Yan, to this day. Larry Yan went on to become a lawyer.

My first task was to teach the Chinese how to write requests for proposals for all the equipment needed for the plant. The Chinese did not have a clue. None of them had ever been trained in competitive bidding. We were able to procure much of the equipment in China. Some had to be shipped in from the United States. I was also expected to liaison with an engineering firm in the USA, which had copies of all the design drawings of ABC Rail's cast steel plant in Calera, Alabama. All these drawings were shipped to Datong. All were redrawn by the Chinese engineers to fit our specific case.

My additional duties were to design and construct a CPM project schedule for the entire project, design a computerized wheel tracking system for the entire casting and machining process, select and install general ledger and accounting systems, and negotiate and select a Chinese engineering firm to assist us in running the project. Such a firm was required by Chinese law.

The firm I selected was a firm headquartered in Beijing named Cerrus. My liaison with the firm was a gentleman by the name of Mr. Shi Shi. He was a great guy. One problem I had was getting my Chinese partners to sign off on contracting with the Beijing engineering firm. I took an overnight train to Beijing to meet secretly with Mr. Shi Shi. I gave him the number he needed to bid to win the project. No other engineering firm (all government owned) were anywhere close in qualifications to the firm I chose. Mr. Shi Shi submitted his bid and his firm won the contract.

Early in the project, we needed to order some long lead time machine tools from the USA. One purchase order was a multimillion-dollar contract. My Chinese counterpart, Mr. Shi, (different guy than Mr. Shi Shi) could not bring himself to countersign the purchase contract. We Americans nicknamed him "Jaime." I signed the purchase order myself as general manager and faxed it to the USA company. The USA company did not know that I was not authorized to sign such a purchase order on my own, but they honored the order and shipped the equipment on time. The Chinese never did sign the purchase order. I learned that the problem with the Chinese was that they learned the hard way that if they took no action, they could not be criticized. The Chinese really feared being criticized.

We had nicknames for most all the Chinese engineers. One we called "Chicken Man" because he was allergic to chicken. Chicken Man turned out to be a snake by stealing all our drawing in an effort to build a carbon copy of our Datong plant elsewhere in China. He failed after a long legal battle. Another two we called "Old Lue" and "Young Lue." Their real names were Mr. Liu and Mr. Liu. The Chinese had difficulty pronouncing the hard "D" in Ned, so I became "Neda." David (Kleeschultee), they could not pronounce at all. His name came out as "Dawie."

During my time in China, an incident occurred which gave me some insight to Chinese thinking. One evening, a group of us Americans were riding back to our housing when an accident ahead of us occurred. Our driver, Mr. King Chui, jumped out of our car and ran to the accident. He came back and said, "He is dead, he is not one of ours, let's go." One dead Chinese made little or no difference to his Chinese mind.

About a year into the project, the wife of one of my Chinese engineers died. At the funeral site, the deceased was laid out in a small building atop a large box. Around the edge of the room were a number of wailing women. In China, the survivors hired "rent-a-mourners." After a brief period of mourning, the deceased was hauled off in a procession to a crematorium. The husband loaded his wife's body into the furnace himself.

Early in the project, we needed to order computer equipment for the general ledger, accounting system, and for the wheel tracking system. Along with my interpreter, I traveled to Beijing where we shopped for computers. When I found the ones I wanted, I purchased them using my credit card. I did not have time to go through the regular company purchasing system. No purchase order was ever prepared. I just bought the damn machines. The company reimbursed me later.

I chuckle as I tell this fun story. The head engineer for our Chinese company partner was a man named Mr. Gao. I really liked the man, but we argued constantly. He was trained by the Russians. Everything had to be massive. On one occasion, we bitterly argued over the design of our plant's dust collection system. When we started negotiations one day, we sat across a long table from each other. As the discussion got louder and louder, I scooted back across the room in my chair. Finally, I told Mr. Gao that I was tired of arguing and asked him to look out the second-story window. Below was a courtyard. I told him I would meet him in the courtyard, and we would settle the argument with fists. That broke up the room in laughter. Eventually, through a bit of subterfuge on my part, my design prevailed.

My time in China was not all work. During the negotiating period from 1993 until 1996, Mr. Zheng, the Chinese leader, invited me and several of my American colleagues when they were in town for dinner in Beijing and Datong. During my nearly two years working full-time in Datong, Mr. Zheng often invited me along with eight or ten Chinese engineers to quite lavish dinners held in private rooms in restaurants around Datong. The dinners were spectacular. One of the delicacies favored by the Chinese was the head of a fish. Because I was the guest of honor, the Chinese would often offer me the fish head. I would dutifully eat the head to the delight of the Chinese. I cannot say that fish heads were my favorite Chinese food. Often after dinner, Mr. Zheng would invite me to ballroom dancing studios around Datong. On several occasions, I had the pleasure of dancing with an older retired lady who had been the champion ballroom dancer in all of China. Always in tow were five or six Chinese engineers and three or four young ladies. Often at the dancing sessions, I would make up Chinese emperor stories for the ladies.

I always included in the story a Cinderella character for the lady's benefit. I became quite a storytelling hit. Other times when we would finish dinner, Mr. Zheng would take us to karaoke clubs. The Chinese loved karaoke. David Kleeschulte, my USA boss, accompanied us on these safaris whenever he was in Datong.

I recall one very special dinner. I asked Mr. Zheng to arrange a dinner with some of the retired military he knew. We had a very nice, but polite dinner. The rule with the Chinese is that the first time one meets one is polite. The second time one meets one is a friend. I asked Mr. Zheng to arrange another dinner at which we would each wear our uniforms. We had a wonderful dinner, and all got quite drunk. Each in turn talked about their military experiences. One related that he had served in Korea and Vietnam. The Korean War vet told me that he always picked up a small piece of wood from each battlefield he was on and from the wood carved a smoking pipe. I smoked pipe at the time. Not long after, the old soldier presented me with a hand-carved pipe. He told me that the wood came from a battlefield in Korea.

The Chinese loved basketball and were quite aware that the Chicago Bulls and Michael Jordan were on a rampage. One year during playoffs, the Chinese arranged for us to watch games live in one of our rooms. There is a twelve-hour time difference between Chicago and Datong, so we watched the games in what was the middle of the night for us.

I brought along with me a computer golf game when I went to Datong. Whenever other Americans were there, we played endless games of computer golf on my computer. Many yuan changed hands on those evenings.

Toward the end of my Datong assignment, my parent USA company sent over a mid-thirties engineer who had been one of the company's plant managers to take over my general manager position when I left. This gentleman prided himself as being a campion table tennis player, so I set up a match between the American braggart and Mr. Zheng. I had the sneaking suspicion that Mr. Zheng was a very good table tennis player. All the Chinese engineers came to watch the match. To induce the Chinese to bet, I gave them ten to one odds that Mr. Zheng would win. Mr. Zheng played with the American for a bit just to make me nervous. The match was no contest. Mr. Zheng could have won twenty-one to zero if he had wanted. I collected my bets and did not have to listen to the American brag about his table tennis skills anymore.

During the contract negotiating phase, 1993–1996, of my efforts on the China project were a lot of fun meetings that involved many trips to Beijing, China, and to Datong, a "small" town of some two million inhabitants. About half of the negotiating meetings were held in the United States.

On a side trip to another town in China named Talien, our negotiating team met with a Chinese railway company which produced railroad Trackwork products. Eventually, we signed a contract with that company, which never resulted in much fruit.

Accompanying David Kleeschultee and me on the Talien trip was a gentleman by the name of John Donovan. John was a husky fellow with crew-cut red hair and a red beard. He had biceps as thick as tree trunks. John was an ex-Green Beret explosive expert who owned a steel hardening company located in the United States. On occasion as a civilian, John was secretly dropped into Afghanistan to blow up Russian things during the Russian invasion of that country.

One night, John and I found ourselves in a small Chinese bar rather late in the evening. After a few beers, we proceeded to leave the bar when we discovered that the Chinese had grossly overcharged us for beer. John and I threw what we thought was a fair amount of cash on the bar and proceeded to walk out. We found ourselves surrounded by Chinese blocking our departure. Each of us grabbed an empty bottle of beer and proceeded back-to-back to make our way toward the bar exit. I was leading, John guarded our rear. When we reached the door, I discovered that the glass door exit was chained shut. I informed John, advising him that I planned to kick out the glass from the door. When the Chinese noticed my intentions, they rushed to the door and removed the chain barring our exit. When the door opened, I looked out onto a cool clear night sky. Outside the door stood a crowd of fifteen or more threatening-looking Chinese men. I really thought that John and I were in a world of hurt. A rather odd thought entered my mind as I looked into the clear night sky and upon what fate awaited me. I said to myself in my own mind,

"Ned, tonight is a good time to die". We walked out of the door. No harm befell us. When John and I returned to our hotel, we drank a few more beers to settle our nerves. Adrenaline slowly ebbed away. That night, in our still drunken stupor, John made me an honorary member of the Green Berets.

The Talien incident recalls to my mind another fatalist event. A Union Switch and Signal fellow employee, Vince Catullo, and I were aboard an aircraft which encountered a mechanical problem. The pilot announced that the landing gear would not lock down. He told us that we would have to make a wheels-up landing. As we approached a foam-covered runway, a stewardess advised us to grab our pillow, bend over, and grasp our legs. I remember turning to Vince as we made our final approach saying, "Vince, it has been nice knowing you." We landed safely and walked away from the aircraft unharmed. When my time really comes, I wonder what my thoughts will be.

During the contract negotiation period, I and a small group of venture capitalists purchased Western Buckle Company located in Chicago, Illinois. Worst deal I ever made. We bought the company at the absolutely wrong time in the Western buckle market. Sales collapsed. We had to close down the plant and sell all the assets. I lost my butt.

Later on, I got involved with a group of businessmen in Chicago on a high- tech project. A friend of mine, Doctor Horn, invented a very clever piece of software to test one's eyes for glaucoma and other eye maladies. The product would have replaced a several thousand-dollar machine used by doctors throughout the world. To advance the project, I hired a recent University of Chicago MBA graduate anesthesiologist to run the project. He blew through in one year more than one hundred thousand dollars, but never produced a business plan to present to investors. The time frame was early 2000. Because of the anesthesiologist's miserable failure to produce an investor proposal, we missed the window of opportunity. The 2000–2001 economy collapse caused venture capital for high-tech projects to dry up. The product could have made millions. Instead, I lost more than one hundred thousand dollars. The worst part is that a few of my friends lost their investments too. Lucky for me, I got the China gig and recovered much of my losses on my two failed projects.

In 1999 or 2000, two of my old friends, Larry DeBoer and Larry Belluchie, and I decided to go on a rafting trip down the Colorado River. We flew to Las Vegas from which we were flown on in a light plane to a landing spot upriver. There, we boarded large Vietnam-era rubber rafts and proceeded thirty miles or so down river. Each lunchtime, we would stop along the way and have a cold lunch provided by the raft crew. During each stop, we would hike up trails leading away from the river. I had just had bypass heart surgery in late 1998, so I felt like I was twenty-five years old. Hiking up steep slopes was no problem for me at all. Each night, we stopped at beautiful, very soft sand beaches to pitch our tents and have dinner cooked by the raft crew. After ten days, we reached the end of the trip. Along the way, we transversed many rapids. Larry and I would always ride in front of the raft, which the crew called the bathtub. Every time we would go over a rapid, Larry and I would get soaked to the skin with very cold water. The air temperature was near one hundred degrees, but the water temperature was about forty degrees. The water was so cold because water was let out of the six- hundred-foot dam upriver at the bottom of the dam. When we got to the last big rapid, I got very wet and very cold. We docked near large black rocks. I climbed up on the rock spread-eagled to get warm. Larry took a picture of that scene.

A year or two after we moved to Port Saint Lucy, Carol and I bought a thirty-six-foot motor yacht. My friend, Steve, and I along with a couple of friends took the boat across Florida on a golfing trip. Each night, we would stop along the canal that goes all the way across Florida to Fort Meyers. Each morning, we would play golf at a local golf course. One morning, we got out on a course about 7:30

in the morning. The day was very foggy. One could not see where one hit one's ball. After a couple of holes, Steve announced that it just was not fair. He could not see his ball. I retorted to Steve, "What the hell makes you think that anyone else can see their ball?" We all had a good laugh. We finished the golfing part and sailed on down to Key West. Steve got very sick and had to fly home. When I got home a few days later, I caught the same bug and spent three days flat on my back. A few months later, Steve borrowed my boat for a cruise with a couple of his friends. They had a devil of a time. One of the diesel engines started to leak oil. They were lucky that they did not get stopped and fined by the Coast Guard.

A few months later, I traded the thirty-six-foot yacht in for a forty-one-foot very nice cabin cruiser. The boat was only about one year old and had been originally bought new by Chi Chi Rodrigues. The cruiser had two very nice cabins. One forward and one aft each with its own full bath. In the midsection of the boat was a large fully equipped kitchen and lounge area. Underneath the deck of the mid galley section were two large Caterpillar diesel engines. The boat was equipped with a complete radar system, an automatic GPS system, a radio system, a depth finder, and a fish finder. Many times, we took a number of our neighbors out for lunch or dinner. On each outing, the ship would burn about fifty dollars' worth of diesel fuel. I do not recall a single time that any passenger ever offered to buy Carol's or my lunch. Oh well.

In about 2001 or 2002, I decided to sail the cruiser to the Thousand Islands along the Saint Lawrence River in upstate New York just across the border from Canada. What a trip that was. My oldest daughter, Carrie, and my young grandson, Jeff Reilly, along with one other crewman accompanied me. We sailed from Florida straight up the Atlantic Ocean toward Cape Fear, North Carolina. I always wondered why the cape was called Cape Fear. At times, we were fifty miles out in the ocean. Each day, we would travel about two hundred miles, then stop at a marina for the night. Until we got to Chesapeake Bay, the weather was very pleasant. Then, a rainstorm and high waves came in. I decided to sail up the bay to the top end where we could cross over to the Delaware Bay and then continue on in Intracoastal Waterways. Part way up the Chesapeake, one of our diesel engines stopped. Carrie grabbed the helm and I jumped below. When I opened the engine hatch, I was shocked by the amount of diesel fuel squirting everywhere. I quickly discovered a broken metal fuel line and quickly shut off the fuel to that engine. I managed to temporarily repair the fuel line and we were able to be on our way. At the next marina we came to, I had the fuel line properly repaired.

We continued to motor up the Intracoastal and eventually came back out to the ocean at the end of the Intracoastal about thirty-five miles south of New York Harbor. We stayed overnight at a last marina in New Jersey. In the early morning, we proceeded out into the Atlantic. Conditions were very foggy. Luckily for us, we had a good radar system so we could see the constant stream of large ocean-going freighters coming toward us. Just as we entered the New York Harbor, the sun came out. We enjoyed the beautiful view of the Statue of Liberty as we passed by. Up on the Hudson River we sailed. Many miles up the river, we entered the Erie Canal. The canal crosses the State of New York all the way to Lake Ontario. Along the canal, we went through many locks. Eventually, we arrived at Lake Ontario. Across, we sailed to our Thousand Islands marina. Carrie and Jeff flew home. Carol flew up to meet me in our Thousand Islands marina. We stayed about one month. Near the end of our Thousand Islands stay, my friend, Larry DeBoer, and his wife Sue flew up to sail back to Florida with us. We had quite a trip. Stubborn as I am, I insisted that we stick with the "float plan" I had prepared for the trip. So, on the float plan set date we raised anchor. Across Lake Ontario we went. Lake water was very rough. Carol noted that all other boats she could see were rapidly headed for shore. I pressed on. We finally safely made our way across the lake. Our trip across Erie Canal was largely uneventful, but quite rainy. When we arrived at the Hudson River, a storm was brewing. We were catching the tail end of a rather severe hurricane, which had clobbered the east coast of the Carolinas. As we proceeded down the Hudson, rain came pummeling down on us and the wind blew about forty miles per hour from our stern. We were traveling about thirty miles per hour. The wind was blowing so hard that the rain was blowing right past us. Eventually, we made it to our planned marina stop. We experienced a very difficult time getting backed into our slip. I nearly wrecked into other boats trying to back into our slip. After four or five tries, we made it. Late that night, everyone in the marina was awakened to grab any available rope and tie off our boats to many large poles, which secured the slip docks. We made it through the night with only one boat rolled up onto the end of our marina. After a day or so, we continued our trip. After many days, we arrived at a South Carolina marina. Just north of the marina, we struck something in the water and broke a propeller. Our air conditioning had failed. The devastation along the Carolina coast was severe. As soon as we docked, Carol pointed out that we were only about two and a half hours from home by car. I said not a word. I went to the nearest telephone where I called for a rent-a-car. Carol and Sue were on their way in minutes. Larry and I stayed on the boat until the propeller could be repaired. A few days later, Larry and I arrived back at my home port.

A couple of years later, Carol and I decided to take our oldest granddaughter, Anne Bendle, on a cruise to the west coast of Florida to Mobile, Alabama, on up the Tom Bigbie waterway to the Mississippi River. Our goal was to reach Pittsburgh, Pennsylvania. We never made it. Just west of Clewiston, Florida, along the Okeechobee Lake Canal, I managed to sink the boat. Coming around a curve, I positioned the boat too close to the rocky south shore. I struck a rock, which drove my portside rudder into the haul. The boat quickly began to sink. In a desperate attempt to avoid going down in the twenty-foot-deep canal, I drove the boat onto the muddy north shore.

The one and only time I ever had the occasion, I took advantage of the incident to shout "Mayday, Mayday" over my on-board radio. Before my engines quit, I managed to get the boat ashore with the bow nearly out of the water and the aft about eight feet underwater. Local Coast Guard folks managed to get Carol and Anne off the boat along with our dogs and one cat. One cat was stuck in the very bow of the boat. I made my way to the bow to fetch the cat. Making my way to the cat along a very slopped deck, I slipped and fell into the engine well. The water was over my head. I managed to swim to the surface and continued toward the cat. I finally clutched the cat in my arm and proceeded to make my way to a place where I could exit the boat. On the way back, the cat and I again slipped into the engine hold. We managed to make it back to the surface and were rescued off the boat. The poor old cat was terrified. Back at the Clewiston marina hotel, I caught up with Carol and Anne. Carol told me that the first thing Anne wanted to do was call her mother and tell her that as soon as she got home, she was going to need a therapist.

But that was not the end of the bad news. At the time of the sinking, a local sheriff deputy met me at the boat and questioned me about what happened. I told him that it was my screwup. The sheriff was an ex-United States Marine. The next day, the ex-marine came by the marina where my boat had been hauled back to and handed me a ticket for failure to pay proper attention. I was ordered to appear in court. The citation was for a misdemeanor felony. I decided to fight. A number of hearings before a judge were scheduled. Each time the judge would ask the ex-marine how he learned of my actions, he told the judge that he had been told the details by a third party. The judge demanded that the third party appear. The ex-marine could not remember the informant's name. Finally, the judge dismissed the case. I dodged another silver bullet and I owe that marine.

The good news was that I had insurance on the boat. The even better news was that because I had owned the boat for over two years, I had decided to reduce the amount of insurance on the vessel. But, luckily for me, the insurance change did not take effect until two weeks after the sinking. As a result, I was paid more for the boat than I could have possibly sold it for. I had planned to sell the boat at the end of this last boating adventure anyway. So, old Ned went out of the boating business. Talk about dodging silver bullets.

I guess because I did not believe I had yet punished myself enough, I decided to go into the "horse business." At our new house in Melbourne, I built a horse barn that included enough space to house my then small-class C RV. My grandson, Jeff, helped lay roof plywood and shingles. I built rest of the barn with my own hands. But I made three mistakes. (1) I built the barn too low to the ground. The first heavy rain, the barn flooded. So, I had to tear up the barn plank floor, pour about six inches of concrete, and relay the floor. My friend, Freddie, helped relaying the wood floor. (2) I did the wiring myself. When I plugged in the RV, poof. Several of the electrical units in the RV blew up. I discovered that I had wired 220 volts into the RV. I hired a real electrician. (3) I neglected to consider the air conditioner atop the RV. So, the RV did not fit under the rafters. Nothing to do but modify the rafter structure to include a slot for the air conditioner.

My daughter, who lived in New Mexico, shipped to me a six-month old Western Mustang. Great horse. His name was Jama. I chose Jama's name to honor my grandchildren, Jeff, Anne, Maddie, and Allen. The horse was like a dog. It followed me all around my pasture as I worked on things. He was constantly looking for a treat, which I often kept in my pocket. When the horse got big enough, I saddled him up and started to ride him. By that time, I had purchased another old trail horse. My friend, Ed Duley, and I would ride the two horses regularly. One day, we were sitting atop our horses at an intersection. Something spoked Jama. Jama sprung out from under me. I fell on my shoulder and broke my collarbone. That was the end of my cowboy days. Not long after, I gave the horse away to a horse rancher near Ocala, Florida. The owner repapered the horse and sold him for five thousand dollars. I learned that the south Florida resident who bought Jama won several awards and eventually sold the horse for ten thousand dollars. I may have run out of silver bullets.

But all was not lost. Carol and I now enjoy traveling around the USA in our forty-one-foot class A RV. We have managed to stay overnight in every one of the lower forty-eight states, except Colorado and Rhode Island (Rhode Island has no RV parks that I know of).

Over the years, I evolved from a liberal-thinking, young college student (as Winston Churchill predicted) to a Constitution conservative. Churchill stated that "When one is twenty years old, if one is not a liberal, one does not have a heart. When one reaches forty years old, if one is not a conservative, one does not have a brain."

In the 1964 Johnson–Goldwater election, I was taken in by Johnson's rhetoric and the Democratic Party's painting of Goldwater as a dangerous candidate. Later, I realized that although Johnson's push to get civil rights legislation through Congress was sorely needed, his Great Society program has been a disaster for the very folks it was intended to help.

I believe that if the democratic socialist have their way, they will bring about the destruction of my beloved country. I cannot understand how the left can reconcile the idea that killing a baby in the womb (in some cases, right up to the moment of birth), yet favor legislation which deems that a drunk driver who kills a woman and her unborn child is guilty of a double homicide. I cannot understand the left's interest in socialism when the evidence is and constitutional republic in favor of socialism when the system put in place by our founders has led to the greatest, most prosperous country in human history. I am dismayed by the steady erosion of our American freedoms brought about by the endless rules and regulations which now thwart our freedom to live our lives as we see fit as an individual. I am dismayed by the steady destruction of the American family unit and the steady encroachment of religious freedom and free speech. I am dismayed by the steady encroachment of the Federal government into nearly every aspect of our lives. I am dismayed by the steady increase of Federal power and the erosion of State and local community powers. I am dismayed that the Progressives have brought all this erosion of freedoms and increased the power of the Federal government at the expense of the States though the ever left-leaning courts. I am dismayed that an increasing number of Americans buy into the Progressive ideas that "free from the Federal government" is the direction our country should proceed. I am dismayed that few if any politicians consider anything but their own interest and power. The people be damned. I am dismayed that much of the liberal press, which is intended to help to keep us free by telling us the truth so blatantly, lies to us. It is no wonder that a majority of Americans no longer trust the press. It is no surprise to me that a majority of Americans no longer trust politicians. I do not understand why the left would junk our capitalistic economic system.

I very much hope that a case will reach the Supreme Court, which will overturn the 1950s law which permits Federal grants to States (with strings attached) "so long as the Federal government does not force the States to accept the funds." It is the Progressive interpretation of this statue that has led to the nearly complete erosion of State responsibilities and the intrusion of the Federal government into many areas our Constitution clearly reserves for the States or the people.

Nowadays, Carol and I live quietly in our nice little house in the mostly military retiree community called Indian River Colony Club. Lucky for us, just down the street is a retirement home. We could crawl that far if the need arises.

CHAPTER 7

My Sister Darlene's Story

Darlene was born on January 12, 1944. She was a very cute little girl. I loved her dearly from the day my mom brought her home to our little house at 736 McCalmont Street. Darlene and I were very close growing up and remain so to this day. I have so many fond memories of our childhood days. One memory, I chagrin to think about and regret ever being so cruel. One Christmas, my older sister Snooky and I decided that Darlene was a bit of a spoiled brat, so I decided to sneak out in the middle of the night and exchange the candy in Darlene's stocking for coal. When Darlene dug into her stocking, she cried. Wish I had not done that. I am truly sorry, Darlene. I was about ten years old at the time.

Truth be told, I am a bit jealous of my sister, Darlene. She is a very good athlete; me, not so much. She could beat me at everything. When Darlene was just a tiny tot, we used to play ping pong on a roughly made tennis table in our basement. For the first few years, I could easily beat her. One day, though, she trounced me soundly. I never played table tennis with her again. To this very day, Darlene in her seventies plays a very mean game of court tennis. Oh well, some folks just have talent.

Darlene grew up to be quite an attractive young lady. I remember how proud of her I was when she became a cheerleader for our basketball team at Rocky Grove High School in our little town of Rocky Grove, Pennsylvania.

Like me, Darlene went on to college at Slippery Rock State Teacher's College (now Slippery Rock University). Darlene majored in physical education and graduated in four years. Following graduation, she married James Riddle, a fellow student at Rocky Grove High School. I always liked Jim, not so much did Darlene whose marriage with Jim eventually failed. I continued to maintain a good relationship with Jim over the years and stay in contact with him to this day. My relationship with Jim deeply troubled Darlene. We had many heated words over the subject and for a time rather drifted apart. But eventually, our love for each other brought us back together.

Jim and Darlene had three sons: James Logan (he prefers to be called Logan), Matthew, and Daniel. Logan is quite a successful accountant. Daniel is a successful television show editor. Dan and his crew have been and continue to be editors on several television shows. Two of my favorites were *Downward Dog* and *My Name Is Earl*. Dan lives and works in California. Mathew, their youngest boy, lives in Arizona.

Late in Jim and Darlene's marriage, Jim got a mechanical engineering assignment to Australia. Darlene has many stories to tell about the great times she enjoyed getting to know the people of Australia. When Jim and Darlene returned to the USA, they built quite a nice house outside of Cleveland, Ohio.

Not long after Darlene and Jim moved back to Cleveland, Darlene divorced Jim and married Craig Coberly. I remember very well those troubled days for Darlene. We often talked about her problems. When she finally decided to leave Jim, she confined to me that the most difficult part was telling our mother and father.

From the day I met Craig, I liked him. He is one of the most honest men I have ever met. Craig is an extremely intelligent man and raised two very successful attorney sons from his marriage to his first wife. One son is married to quite a successful lawyer in Chicago. The other lawyer son practices law in Santa Fe, New Mexico. Craig's Santa Fe son recently made his debut presenting a case before the United States Supreme Court.

Craig and Darlene have now been married over twenty-five years and continue to enjoy life together. Craig's two sons have blessed Darlene and Craig with grandchildren. The children spend considerable time visiting Darlene and Craig in Florida.

When Darlene was still young, she joined Delta Airlines and had quite a successful career with the company. Her last assignment was as a Red Coat customer service supervisor at the Atlanta airport. Darlene retired several years ago and nowadays, Craig and Darlene enjoy the airline employee perk of mostly free flights around the world. They regularly flit about the world enjoying the perk. I am jealous. Just kidding, Darlene.

After Darlene retired from Delta, she moved to Venice, Florida, built a lovely house, and enjoys much the retired life in their idyllic town. Quite often, we visit Craig and Darlene in Venice, and they visit us in Melbourne, Florida.

Carol and I, for many years, have enjoyed RV'ing about the country. Last year, Craig entertained the idea of buying an RV. I told them that they were welcome to use our class A RV anytime they wished. Carol and I only use the RV a couple of months each year. For a test run, I invited Darlene and Craig to go on a trip from Melbourne to St. Augustine, Florida. Craig drove the whole way up to St. Augustine and back and learned the ins and outs of RV'ing. Darlene and Craig fell in love with traveling about in an RV, so they decided to take me up on my offer the next summer. Now, Darlene and Craig are hooked, so they plan to use our RV for a month or two each summer.

Recently, Craig and Darlene offered to remodel the inside of our RV as a way of thanking us for letting them use our RV. They cleaned up the window treatments, removed carpeting and replaced it with wood flooring, installed bench seats for the kitchen table, and resurfaced all countertops. They finished all the remodeling work in February 2019. The two of them did an incredibly nice job of remodeling. When Carol and I drove to Venice to pick up our RV, we were more than a little impressed. The inside of the RV looks like new. Craig, being quite the craftsman, did most of the remodeling work. Darlene contributed by doing a great job of choosing color schemes and thoroughly cleaning the RV. Craig tells me that Darlene closely supervised all his work. When he completed a task, Darlene inspected his work. If the work was not up to Darlene's high standards, she demanded that Craig tear his work out and redo it until he "did it right." Thank you, Darlene and Craig. The work you did is truly beautiful. Carol and I could not have been more pleased with the color scheme and the craftsman's attention to detail.

Rumors are that Ned Cole will soon be indicted for engaging in slave labor.

Carol and I planned an April RV visit to our long-ago air force days at the Keesler AFB in Biloxi, Mississippi, and a June–July trip to visit Revolutionary battlefields where our ancestors fought. Darlene and Craig plan a trip for a month or so in July and August next summer. We made that trip.

CHAPTER 8

Carol's Story

Mary Carol Vensel Cole was born on April 21, 1941, in Butler, Pennsylvania, to Elsie Mae (Hegburg) and James Browning Vensel. Her grandmother, Hegburg, was also named Mary, so her family called her "Carol." Her grandfather, Hegburg, was born in Sweden in the mid-1800s. He died in 1956. Her grandmother, Mary Hegburg, after whom Mary Carol was named, was born in Reynoldsville, Pennsylvania, on September 30, 1879. Mary Hegburg died on January 16, 1976. In grade school and high school, Carol, was known as "Mary Carol." To everyone else in her life, she is just "Carol" and introduces herself that way.

Carol was a very pretty, little blond-haired, blue-eyed girl. She grew into quite a pretty adult woman. Carol was an outstanding student in grade school and high school. She spent her first few years in two one-room schoolhouses, Pipestem and Coaltown, Pennsylvania, near West Sunbury, Pennsylvania. She quickly became her teachers' star pupil. Her teachers often enlisted Carol to help teach the younger children.

Carol had one sister, Judy, who was about four years younger.

Carol spent her high school days at Moniteau High School in Hooker, Pennsylvania. (I am told that graduates from that high school are called "Hookers." The subject is not one of Carol's favorites.) Her class was the last one to graduate from the old building. The next year, the high school moved to a newly consolidated school located at the north end of West Sunbury, Pennsylvania. She graduated second in her high school class. I completed a student teacher semester at the new Moniteau High School in the fall of 1960. Upon graduation from high school in 1959, Carol enrolled in college at Slippery Rock Teachers College, now called Slippery Rock University, where she majored in English. She paid for her college education by babysitting, working as a nurse's aide, small scholarships, and small loans.

Carol met her husband-to-be, Ned M. Cole Jr., in her freshman year at Slippery Rock. They were married on May 3, 1961, in Cumberland, Maryland. Carol was twenty years old and Ned was twenty-one years old. Their first child, Carrie, was born prematurely just before Christmas. Carol had considerable difficulty with her three pregnancies. Carrie's birth was extremely difficult. After twelve hours of painful labor, Carol determined that Carrie was the first and last child she would ever have. Ned agreed. Nearly four years past before the memories of Carrie's painful birth faded enough for Carol to again consider pregnancy. Regina and Jeff were very difficult pregnancies for Carol to carry to term. Neither made it to term, but both popped out with little difficultly.

When Ned graduated college in January 1962, the small family moved to Addison, New York, where Ned was hired as a ninth-grade teacher. Carol suspended her college career for a few years.

Although Carol worked at several jobs during her marriage to Ned, her most important job was always to be a stay-at-home mom where she could dedicate herself to raising her five children. Caring for and raising five children was more than a full-time job. Many times, Ned credited his success in business to Carol. Ned understood that without her dedication to family, he would never have been able to devote as much energy to his business career. His career took him all over the world, often for months at a time. Having a great wife who always covered the home front made it all possible.

After a few years and when her five children were out of diapers, Carol returned to college and finished her bachelor's at Chatham College, an all- women's college in Pittsburgh, Pennsylvania. During her Chatham days, Carol chose for her bachelor "dissertation" a study of deaf children education at the Pittsburgh School for the Deaf. At the time, the school did not know that Carol was the mother of a deaf child. Her final report was extremely critical of how the school educated deaf children. As a result of her report and her active participation in deaf organizations, the Pennsylvania Department of Education was forced many changes at the school.

In August 1962, Ned enlisted in the United States Air Force and flew off to San Antonio for Officers Training School at Lakeland Air Force base. Carol stayed at home with her parents and continued taking classes at Slippery Rock.

When Ned finished OTS, he was ordered to Biloxi, Mississippi, where he enrolled in the USAF Communications Electronics forty-three-week school. Carol joined him there.. At Keesler AFB, the couple was assigned an on-base cozy brick duplex.

When Ned was reassigned to Westover AFB in Springfield, Massachusetts the family moved to Old Orchard, a suburb of Springfield. Base housing was not available. The house they moved into was rented to them by the family who owned the house. The owner occupied the second floor. The Coles occupied the first floor. The house had a coal-fired furnace. All of the walls were covered in black soot. When Carol saw what was to be her home, she cried. In short order, Ned covered the blackened walls with a fresh coat of paint and bought a used washer and dryer. Carol's morale considerably improved. Because they could not afford rental costs on Ned's second lieutenant salary, Carol had to return to work. She worked nights as a nurse's aide at the Springfield Hospital, while Ned worked days at Westover AFB. They passed in their front doorway each morning and evening.

After less than a year breathing coal dust, Carol and Ned bought a small single-family house near the main gate of Westover AFB. They paid nine thousand five hundred dollars for the house with minimal down payment under the terms of a VA loan. The house was a dirty gray but was soon painted a clean white. When Ned was promoted to first lieutenant and went over two years in service, Carol was able to quit working as a nurse's aide. In 1965, Carol gave birth to their second child.

After about two years at Westover, Ned was reassigned to Offutt AFB, Omaha, Nebraska. The young couple rented a nice house from one of the civilians working in the same office as Ned.

Carol began to make friends with military wives and will tell you today that she rather enjoyed the family's time in the military.

The family stayed in Omaha for about two years until Ned was discharged from the air force. Carol and their baby daughter flew back to Rocky Grove, Pennsylvania, to live with Ned's mother and father for a short time. Ned followed with Carrie a few days later. All of their household goods were packed in their tiny Nash Rambler.

A month or so after discharge from the USAF in fall of 1967, the family moved to Fitzwatertown Road, Roslyn, Pennsylvania, when Ned was hired by Auerbach Corporation located in downtown Philadelphia. They bought a nice two-story colonial house and settled in to enjoy civilian life. In November 1967, Carol gave birth to their third child, a son, Jeffrey.

A rather fun for the Cole's incident occurred when they lived at the Fitzwatertown house. Unknown to Ned and Carol, the back of their lot contained a water-flow easement. The land from the back of their house sloped gradually upward to a neighbor's house about fifty yards away. The neighbor complained about what he perceived to be a possible flooding problem. The problem made its way to the county government. The county, citing a drainage easement in the back of our house, demanded that they correct the problem. They contacted a crusty old lawyer who played their title insurance company like the first violinist at the New York Philharmonic. The title company had missed the easement when underwriting their title insurance. The title company paid in excess of ten thousand dollars and their lawyer fees to relandscape their property. The Coles "dodge a silver bullet"; Ned's silver bullet gene was functioning well.

But they also had a disturbing event at Fitzwatertown. One late evening, they heard a car crash near their house. They ran out to find an upside-down convertible and a very dead young man lying next to their curb.

After less than two years, the family moved to Murrysville, Pennsylvania, when Ned was hired by Union Switch and Signal located in Swissvale, Pennsylvania.

In late 1972 Carol and Ned brought Jonathan Ned Cole, a biracial baby, into their home, and when the law permitted, adopted Jon about six months later. In 1974, another biracial baby, Benjamin, came to their home, and he, too, was adopted. When Jonathan became old enough to attend school, Carol got a job driving Jon and other handicapped kids to school and returned to college to finish her bachelor's degree in English at Chatham College, Pittsburgh, Pennsylvania. Ned remembers the long nights that Carol spent studying. She always was an outstanding student. In fact, Ned has to confess that he stole some of her study methods in his academic endeavors.

The family lived in Murrysville for ten or eleven years when, in 1980, Ned was transferred to New York City. The family moved to Denville, New Jersey, where they bought a two-story colonial style house in a nice bedroom community. Carol continued her work raising their five children, while Ned continued on with my business career.

In 1982, the family moved to Glenview, Illinois, when Ned was hired by Railroad Products Group, Abex Corporation. With Carrie leaving the nest in New Jersey and the other children grown to young teenagers and beyond, Carol became a real estate agent. For the next ten years, the family lived in Glenview during which time, Ned traveled around the world, while Carol held down the home front.

In 1962, Ned retired from the then ABC Rail Company, and the family moved to Placitas, New Mexico. By then, only Jon, Ben, and Jeff remained in the nest. Jon went off to college, and Jeff stayed at their house while attending University of New Mexico. The family lived there for about five years. For a couple of those years, the family split their time between their Placitas home and a new home in Port St. Lucie, Florida. After about five years shuttling between New Mexico and Florida, the family sold their Placitas home and took up full-time residence in Florida. By this time, only Jon remained at home with his mom and dad. The other kids were scattered about the USA. Carol became quite involved with her church and became the chair of the board of deacons.

Sadly, in 1998, Jonathan died. Carol and Ned went into a year-long extremely depressing period. Eventually, Carol recovered and went on with her life. In 2001, the Cole family sold their Saint Lucie River house where Jon died and moved to Melbourne, Florida. Carol became very active in the Daughters of American Revolution, New England Women, and Daughters of Union Veterans. In turn, she became the leader of each. After a few years living at their "horse ranch" on Tuscawillow Drive in Melbourne, they moved to Indian River Colony Club, a mostly retired military person country club setting where they reside today. Carol continues to be active in her several organizations and continues her efforts to chart family ancestry. She stays busy.

Carol is an avid reader. As long as Ned has known her, she has read about one book a week, sometimes two. Her passion has become early history of America and the many characters who played a role in their country's founding. But her reading interests cover many other historical periods, modern American and world history, and many other subjects. For fun, she reads an endless variety of Agatha Christie-type novels. Murder mystery novels seem to be her favorites. Ned read many books too, but not even close to Carol's league. At Carol's bidding, they have hundreds of books in the library of their house. They occasionally buy hardcover books. Nowadays, they often download books onto their Kindle readers. Their old eyes find it a bit easier to read the "large as one wants print" Kindle readers, but they just cannot resist buying a real book which they can hold in their hands. Their library of hard copy books continues to overflow their library shelves.

At a young age, Carol learned to play piano. When she was young, she played for many years in her local church. In one of the early Christmases, they spent as a married couple, Ned purchased for Carol an upright piano. They gave the upright piano to their daughter, then purchased a white baby grand piano that found its way into their current home. Rarely does Carol play when Ned is around. She tells Ned that she does play when only their two dogs are around to listen.

Carol's mother and father were married in Chicora, Pennsylvania, on February 3, 1940. Carol's father, James Vensel, died of a heart attack at the young age of fifty-nine. He was born on May 28, 1915. He died in 1974.

Carol's father dreamed of going to college to study architecture. James' father had different ideas. His father insisted that James go to work at Armco Steel where he was a superintendent. James, being a bit stubborn, , instead went to work at Pullman Standard where he worked throughout World War II. His plan was to earn enough money to pay his own way through college. But he met Elsie. They got married and started to have children. That ended his college dreams. Unfortunately for James, he developed a thyroid problem and had to leave the factory. He took up farming at a fifty-acre farm in West Sunbury, Pennsylvania. To supplement his meager farming earnings, he took on part-time carpentry work. Eventually, he gave up farming and became a full-time carpenter. That was as close as he could come to his dream of designing skyscrapers. James was well known in his community for his honesty and very good work. He was a very smart young man, but stubborn to his own detriment and difficult to work for. Consequently, he mostly worked alone, thus it limited his earnings. Nevertheless, he made sure that his two daughters got to college. But, like his father before him, he had his ideas about what his daughters should study at college. He insisted that Carol become a teacher rather than the fashion designer she always dreamed of becoming.

Carol's mother, Elsie (Hegburg) Vensel, was born in Butler County, Pennsylvania, on June 24, 1917. She died in Melbourne, Florida, on January 9, 2005, after many years at her own home in West Sunbury, Pennsylvania, a few years in a subsidized apartment, and extended stays in Florida assisted living and nursing homes. Elsie never remarried after her husband died. During the twenty-five years after the death of Elsie's Jimmy, Carol was the steadfast caregiver all those years. Elsie was a homemaker all her adult life.

Carol is descended from a long line of Revolutionary War and Civil War veterans, hence, her active involvement in the Daughters of the American Revolution, Daughters of Civil War Veterans, and New England Women. Carol has great stories to tell about her storied ancestors. Ned hopes that one day she tells that story.

CHAPTER 9

My Son Jonathan Ned Cole's Story

A TALE OF SILENCE

Jon built a tower so that he could see over the trees. He seemed not aware and for sure not concerned that the floor of the forest was crawling with things that would cause him pain.

Jonathan Ned Cole was born on July 6, 1972, to a white-skinned mother and a dark-skinned father. They abandoned him. He was a beautiful child. And though proof of his beauty was not needed for even the casual observer, Jon was named the 1976 National Poster Child for the Deaf.

From birth, Jon was profoundly deaf. He never heard music, the chirping of birds, the rushing of waves, or the cooing of his mother. Jon signed with his little fingers when asked if he was deaf without understanding what deaf means. From his vantage above the trees, he smiled at the sights surrounding him. He did not know and seemed never to imagine that he was doomed. Jon's life ended in a somber retreat from living by a tragic event that need not have happened. Jon was twenty-six years old.

Happy that the Christmas event was near, Jon returned from a Christmas shopping spree to the home of his adoptive parents who were far distant in Chicago visiting friends. He was sure that the gifts so carefully selected would bring joy to his mom and dad and to his siblings, Carrie, Regina, Jeff, and Ben, when they opened their surprises on Christmas Day. Jon loved his family with all his heart.

As he joyously greeted his dog, Pepper, and his cat, Koko, he carried his gifts of love from his red Ford Mustang to his mom's office hideaway, where he was sure he would find a stash of festive Christmas wrappings. Remembering his mom and dad's admonition, "Close the door, Jon," he lumbered back to the garage to press the garage door's down button. Jon was partly paralyzed on his right side from a serious automobile accident three years earlier. Walking was a chore for Jon.

As he watched the door close, he wondered why other people often startled with the first clank of the closing door. But Jon was deaf, you know. The soft sound of the red Ford Mustang's motor running blended with the noise of the door closing. But Jon heard none of this. He only saw. There is nothing to see of a car running.

With his Christmas packages deposited in his mom's packing room, Jon's thoughts became the rumblings of hunger in his stomach. Hunger you feel. Hearing is not important. Pepper and Koko looked with expectant eyes. They heard the rumblings. With a kind stroke of Pepper's head and a gentle pull-on Koko's tail, Jon lumbered with his cane to the pantry where his mom kept a seemingly endless supply of Mighty Dog and Fancy Feast. He laughed the sound that only deaf can make as Pepper and Koko eagerly watched as he dished out the food into their separate bowls. Pepper and Koko waited patiently for they knew that Jon, once a strapping six-foot athlete of a man, had only his left hand to scoop out the food. His right hand remained curled and limp at his chest where it had been since that fateful drive on the road from Albuquerque to Roswell that took away forever his skiing and skateboarding joys. But that story is for another time.

Jon loved boiled Oscar Mayer hot dogs. Bun only, please. No condiments. He smiled as he remembered his mom. She, he knew, was the one who magically kept a supply of Oscar Mayers always on hand. While the water boiled, Jon watched with amusement as the Dr. Pepper fizzled up the side of his glass. Life was a joy with so many things to see from the top of the forest.

The red Ford Mustang purred softly as it spit out its deadly invisible stream.

With a click, the big screen TV kicked on. Ah, the joys of captioned television. A Dr. Pepper in hand, a nibble on an Oscar Mayer, a vibrating cat (cats vibrate when they purr, you know), a soft, curling, little old dog, and the Jetsons for a laugh. What a joy life is. Soon, Mom and Dad will be home. Soon, Carrie, Regina, Jeff, and Ben will come from far away. My gifts are sure to make my family so happy. Christmas is near.

The red Ford Mustang continued its deadly chore. The Mustang screamed out in silence, "But for a small digital chip to automatically shut me down, I would not do this. Jon loves me. I was his gift for graduating from college. Please, I beg you."

The focus on the television is blurring. Please, dear God, do not take my sight away too. Pepper, wake up. Koko, why have you fallen to the floor. My car! Dear God, help me. I read about the deadly fumes. Get up, Jon. Oh, Mom will be angry with me for knocking Great-grandpa's picture off the garage hallway wall. Help me, dear God. The door. I can see the door to the garage. Must shut off the car. Cannot. The marble floor feels so cold. Help me, Mom. And then Jon died.

Ned M Cole, Jr.

Jonathan Ned Cole
July 6, 1972–December 6, 1998.
We love you with all our hearts.

I spoke the following eulogy at Jon's funeral on December 9, 1998. When I finished, my eyes were filled with tears. I was barely able to finish. The packed gathering of friends and family sat silent in their seats crying too. That day was the saddest day of my life.

"Jonathan Ned Cole, our son and the brother of Carrie, Regina, Jeffrey, and Benjamin, was born on July 6, 1972. His life was at once a story of great tragedy for him and a defining joy for those of us who were fortunate enough to know and love him.

"Jon came on this earth only to be abandoned as a baby by those who gave him life. On the most defining day of our lives, six months after his birth, we, his adoptive mom, dad, sisters, and brothers, were blessed to bring him into our family as one of us. In profound ways, Jon taught each of us lessons of life that shall remain with us forever.

"By the time Jon was ten months old, we learned the sad truth that our son was profoundly deaf and had been so since birth. He never heard the soothing of his mother's song, the sound of music, or the comfort of another human being's voice. We learned, in one of those profound lessons of life, that as great as were the injustices of racial inequality with which we as a family struggled for all the years of Jon's life, the pain of struggling with the silence of deafness was even harder to bear.

"Yet, Jon, among all of us, overcame the pain and the loss, and the injustice, and taught us all, his family and nearly all those who had the immeasurable good fortune to be touched by his life, that more important than all of this was the great joy of loving and knowing that one is loved. To Jon, his love of and for his family was everything.

"*Struggling against nearly impossible odds, because he wanted his family to be proud of him, Jon triumphed over his deafness, debilitating asthma, and a terribly tragic automobile accident that left him partly paralyzed for life. He overcame all this to achieve one of his lifelong dreams of completing a college degree. In June 1997, Jon realized his dream and became one of the few totally deaf people to ever stand so proudly in graduation exercises at the Eastern New Mexico University at Roswell. He was so happy, and we were so proud for him.*

"*Even a greater dream for Jon was coming home to his family after years and years of having to be away to educate himself. In June of 1997, Jon finished his coursework and finally came home. For a year, his mom and I had him all to ourselves. What a joy for us after so many years of feeling so sad that we had to send him away for so much of his life.*

"*Jon was finally home with his mom, dad, dog, and cat, never to have to go way again. Seeing his joy of finally being home gave us tears of love every day.*

"*Jon continued with his dreams, his dream of getting a good job in his chosen field of computer science, being able to afford a house of his own, and starting to build his own little family. But who would hire a deaf, physically handicapped young man? Many times, his mother and I nearly gave up hope, but not Jon. There never was a doubt in his mind that he would achieve his goal. Jon could only imagine the good side of it all. Never once did he not believe that justice in the world would see to it that he got a job, found a wife, and had his own children. Never once did he believe that perhaps life was not always fair and kind.*

"*But his dreams were not to be, after all. On December 6, 1998, in a tragic accident, Jon and his beloved animals died.*

"*Oh, Jon, Jon, we miss you so, we are so sorry, but please know that there will never be a greater joy for us than the gift of your love and your life. Your family loves you and will be indebted to you forever for the joy and love you brought to all of us.*"

Ned M Cole, Jr.

December 6, 1998, is a day that continues to echo and reecho in my mind. Even now, nearly twenty-one years later, I cannot talk about Jon without choking back tears. Many times throughout my career when tough times would fall upon me, I would look at the picture of Jon that I always kept on my desk and say to myself, "Ned, if you never do another thing in your life, you will always be able to think of Jon and know that you did at least one good thing." When Jon died, I lost my anchor in life.

The obituary on his death was brief: "Jonathan Ned Cole, twenty-six, of Port St. Lucie, died Sunday, December 6, 1998, at his home. He was born on July 6, 1972, in Allegheny County, Pennsylvania, and had been living with his parents in Port St. Lucie while he sought employment in the computer field. He was a graduate from the Illinois School for the Deaf, attended the National Technical Institute for the Deaf at Rochester, New York, and in 1997, graduated with an associate degree in computer information systems from Eastern New Mexico University, Roswell, New Mexico. He was a volunteer in the circulation department at the Martin County Library, Stuart, Florida.

"Survivors at the time included his parents, Ned M. and Mary Carol Cole, of Port St. Lucie; two brothers and two sisters, Carrie Lynn Cole of Albuquerque, New Mexico, Regina Cole Bendle of Pendleton, Indiana, Jeffrey James Cole of Naperville, Illinois, and Benjamin Don Cole of Albuquerque, New Mexico; paternal grandmother, Evelyn Murrin Cole of Franklin, Pennsylvania; maternal grandmother, Elsie Hegburg Vensel of Slippery Rock, Pennsylvania; and four nieces and nephews."

Since our son died, we have learned that accidental death by carbon monoxide poisoning from a forgotten car is not an isolated event. We have been told that at least six other cases have occurred in Florida alone in the past few years.

Two years after the statute of limitations on such things had run out, I wrote a letter to Ford Motor Company explaining that they need not fear a suit. I told them of the accident and suggested how a simple twenty-five-cent chip could solve the problem. I never got a response from Ford. How many people will have to die before Ford and the other automobile manufacturers do the right thing?

CHAPTER 10

Major USMCR My Oldest Grandson's Story

Jeff A Reilly was born November 3, 1988 to Carrie Cole and William Reilly.

He is our first grandchild. Lucky for me, I was able to spend a considerable amount of time with Jeff when he was growing up.

When Jeff was just a little guy, his mother, Carrie, and dad, Bill Reilly, moved from New Jersey to Albuquerque, New Mexico. My wife, Carol, and I moved from Glenview, Illinois, to a little town twenty-five miles north of Albuquerque called Placitas. We had built our dream house about fifteen miles north of where Carrie and Jeff lived. Carol and I visited the Reillys often and they visited us. At the time we built our house, Carrie owned and operated a high-end bathroom fixture store. All the kitchen and bathroom equipment used in our new house, we purchased from Carrie's store.

Jeff was a builder of forts from the time he was little. He and his local buddies had one under construction in the front of his house most of the time. When he got a bit older, he purchased an old Mustang and practically rebuilt it. He became quite a good mechanic in the process. As a young kid, Jeff started working with his father, Bill, who was a licensed general construction contractor in the Albuquerque area. Jeff became quite talented at home remodeling under his father's guidance.

In 1996, I got a contract to work in Datong, PRC. In 1997, Jeff and his mother traveled to China where they spent two weeks touring the country. Jeff and his mother were quite the hit with the Chinese people. Jeff was nine years old at the time. mother flew to Beijing to visit me for two weeks or so. Jeff's blond hair and blue eyes were quite a hit with the Chinese people. Many families were thrilled when we permitted them to take a picture of their children with Jeff. I do not remember that we ever turned down a request.

A few years later, about 2001 or 2002, I decided to sail my diesel engine yacht from Florida to Thousand Islands on the St. Lawrence River. Jeff and Carrie came along as my crew. What a trip that was. We sailed a couple miles each day stopping a marines each night. By the time we got to the Chesapeake Bay we had to leave the ocean for the bay because of bad weather. Part way up the bay one engine stopped. I rushed to the engine room below deck while Carrie manned the helm. Deisel fuel was flying about. I managed to turn off the diesel supply to that engine. I quicky rigged a temporary fix for the diesel line. We continued our way north. At our next marina stop I had the line properly repaired.

When Jeff was a teenager, he visited me in Melbourne, Florida, and helped me build a horse barn. Jeff was quite an accomplished carpenter and a good worker. His dad, Bill Reilly, taught him well.

As soon as Jeff entered ninth grade, he joined the US Marine Corps Jr. ROTC program. From very early on, Jeff wanted to be a marine. He was quite aware of my longtime military service and I often related to him that at one time I wanted to be a marine. I like to think that my example had some influence on Jeff.

After high school, Jeff enrolled in the University of New Mexico Navy ROTC program. Most years when I could, I flew to Albuquerque for the annual Marine Corps ball. (About 1996 or 1997, Carol and I moved from Placitas to Florida.) Jeff was a very handsome young man. I remember one Marine Corps ball when he danced with four or five very good-looking girls at the same time. Jeff was a good dancer. I think he got that gene from me. In my day, I could cut quite a rug.

I flew to Albuquerque along with Carrie and Maddie for Jeff's commissioning ceremony as Second Lieutenant USMC.

Jeff was shipped off in the summer of 2009 to Officers Candidate School (OCS) at Quantico, Virginia. Carol, Carrie, and I drove to Virginia to watch him graduate from that military training course. He later completed Basic School, Infantry Officers Course, and Scout Sniper unit leader's course. Following the sniper training, he completed the Ground Intelligence Officer Course (SSULC).

After finishing OCS, Jeff cobbled up some cash and traveled around Europe. Jeff made friends everywhere he went, especially girls, so he was able to bunk at his friends' houses along the way. Mostly, though, he stayed at youth hostels around Europe. After six weeks or so, he returned home. His great-great-grandpa Cole would have been proud of him.

After finishing training, Jeff was deployed to Okinawa, Japan, where he stayed for much of his active-duty time. For a couple of months, he was deployed to Australia to work with an Australian unit. He brought back many stories from his time there. After volunteering many times, he got an assignment to Afghanistan. Jeff had some harrowing times to tell about his time in combat. He told me that his most frustrating issue with combat service was the rules of engagement. He told me about one occasion when he and his unit were under 12.7 mm machine gun fire from an enemy positioned in a small building. His marines were not able to return fire due to the rules of engagement. He told me that infiltrators to their compound were a constant worry. On one occasion, one of his Afghan police advisors blew his own hands off trying to kill the Nawzad district chief of police. Jeff carried the Afghan fellow to an aid station. Jeff told me that he never suspected the police officer and quite liked the guy.

All the while that Jeff was on active duty, I regularly sent him a "care" package filled with goodies I thought he would like. Jeff told me that when he received the packages, he set them out on a table in his hooch for his troopers to enjoy. Within minutes, all the goodies would disappear. His grandpa became a rather popular fellow with Jeff's marine comrades.

At the end of his active-duty tour, Jeff came up for what the marines call "career designation." Due to the many Marine Corps cutbacks during President Obama's administration, Jeff was not so designated. Consequently, he was mustered out of active duty. For a short time, he contracted to serve in the Congo as a game warden. Of course, he promptly got malaria and was laid up for a while. After a few months, he returned home to his mother's ranch and helped with keeping the ranch going. All the while, he kept looking for a job. He finally landed one and moved to Virginia.

In the meantime, he met Charlotte, who was quite a successful young woman in her business area. In September 2017, Jeff married Charlotte. Jeff was in his Marine Corps uniform, as were many of his Marine Corps buddies. who participated in the wedding who participated in the wedding.

Charlotte and Jeff bought a house in Alexandria, Virginia. His carpentry skills came in handy as he worked his way through several remodeling projects. One of the projects he completed was to finish his basement as an apartment. They regularly rent out the apartment to transient customers. Charlotte commutes to WDC for her job. For Jeff's civilian job, he can mostly work from home.

While living in Virginia, Jeff secured a billet as platoon commander of a Marine Corps unit headquartered in Harrisburg, Pennsylvania. He and his unit were sent to the Ukraine for exercise Sea Breeze in 2018. His deployments make it difficult for Jeff to keep up with his MBA program. Currently, Jeff and Charlotte are looking for a vineyard to purchase. They hope one day to go into the wine-making business. Charlotte and Jeff's first choice for engaging in the wine-making business was Virginia. But after discovering that because of the climate in Virginia, successful grape growing requires a great deal of pesticides. Now, the couple is considering moving to Texas where grape growing requires fewer pesticides. Then since bought two more houses in Alexandra, Virginia. They rent out this house to government worker. They live in the third house which is situated on a lovely three-acre plot. Jeff continues to remodel that house.

Jeff told me about one deployment to Twentynine Palms which, if memory serves me right, was while he was the platoon commander of a Marine Corps unit. He told me that he had the most fun and at the same time was the most miserable of any deployment he could remember. The temperature reached 130 degrees Fahrenheit. His platoon was tasked with reducing three objectives manned by the "enemy" and then occupying the objectives. Using live motor fire and live covering fifty machine gun fire over the heads of his attacking platoon, his platoon proceeded to fulfill their mission. On the last motor barrage of the third objective, Jeff ordered his motormen to fire all remaining twelve motors. Then, under the cover of white phosphorous, his platoon attacked the third objective and secured it. His platoon finished first in the exercise.

Recently, Jeff told me that trying to maintain a full-time job, commanding an often-deployed marine unit and completing his MBA program was becoming more and more difficult. His current plans are to take a break from the marines at least until he finishes his MBA program. Jeff continues to keep his eyes open for better job opportunities in the civilian area. And his mother tells me that he started working on a book of his own. Jeff finished his MBA at Georgetown University. He paid his way but now struggles to pay off his massive debt. He secured a good job at the Pentagon in intelligence.

CHAPTER 11

My Granddaughter Anne's Story

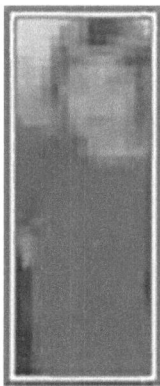

Anne Spencer Bendle was born July 4, 1991 to Regina Cole Bendle and Scott Bendle. At the time Carol and I were traveling through the area and just happened to stop by the hospital where Anne was being born just minutes before her mother gave birth. Carol observed Anne's delivery. I had just settled into a waiting grandpa area when Carol rushed out to tell me that we had a granddaughter. Anne was a very cute, little blond-haired, blue-eyed girl who grew into a quite pretty young woman.

About when she 16 years old, she decided to move to Florida to attend Florida Air Academy. Her first semester she stayed on campus along with her two-year younger cousin, Madeline Cole. The remainder of her time at Florida Air she stayed at our house in Melbourne. Anne was a good student. At the Academy she met

Vincent (Vinnie_ Iorio whom she later married. After she graduated from Florida Air she attended college for a time. She did not do well at college. She was forced to drop out. Anne then decided on a nursing career and quickly finished nurse's training. She is now employed in her chosen field. Shortly after finishing nurses training she married her longtime friend, Vinnie.

They have one son who is a ball of energy.

CHAPTER 12

My Granddaughter Madeline's Story

Maddie was born on <u>April 29, 1994</u> in Albuquerque, New Mexico. Maddie was born to her mother's second husband. I have a picture of Maddie and my sister, Snooky, when both were about six years old. If one were to place the pictures side by side, one would be hard-pressed to tell one from the other.

Maddie was a quiet little girl and good student. She seemed to have learned early in life that one's ears never get one in trouble, but one's mouth is a different story.

Maddie graduated from Florida Air Academy where she met her first husband. After graduation she entered a hair dressing program. They were married when Maddie turned 18 years old. Shortly after marriage her husband joined the United States Air Force. Ater his basic training they moved to his new assignment at Mountain Home

Air Force Base, Idaho. Not long after he decided he did not want to be married. He put Maddie on a plane with no money and little more than the clothes on her back. Soon after they were divorced.

After returning home to her mother in Holapaw, Florida, she began a teacher training program. She is now employed as a grade schoolteacher. She specializes in troubled children.

She married Corey Berg, a successful computer hardware repairman. They soon bought a house in Florida near where they work.

CHAPTER 13

My Grandson Allen's Story

Allen Bendle was born May 13, 1997 in <u>Hamilton Indiana</u>. After graduating from high school, he continued his academics. In June 2019, he graduated with a bachelor's degree in political science. He now works in Chicago, Illinois.

In Chicago he met a lovely young woman named Audrey Flood. They are considering marriage. Both have successful careers.

CHAPTER 14

Michael, My First Nephew's Story

Michael was born in September 1998 in Franklin, Pennsylvania to my sister, Snooky, and Pat Karns.

He was the first grandchild born in the Ned and Evelyn Cole's family.

After Michael graduated from high school, he enlisted in the United States Army. His MOS was tank operator.

On his first overseas assignment, Michael was stationed in Germany. While there, he had the occasion to meet many German soldiers. One day, he met a German general. According to Mike, they had a "nice chat." The German general tagged him "Feldher." The nickname stuck with him.

After leaving the US Army, Michael worked his way through college and became a computer intelligence expert. Soon, he moved to Washington, DC, where he worked for a contractor that was engaged in various cyber activities for the government.

Michael told me that one day, while he was at an ATM with a friend, they were held up at gunpoint. His friend was shot. Michael was uninjured. Not long after that incident, Michael returned home to Rocky Grove, Pennsylvania, to be near his parents. Mike's mother and father were getting quite old.

When Mike first returned to Rocky Grove, he signed on as the financial controller of Sugar Creek Township He found a number of irregularities. The county panicked. They fired him. Michael was and is absolutely uncorruptible.

As a Rocky Grove Fire Department volunteer, he took over straightening out their books. He quickly found irregularities. They told him to go away.

Michael continues a lively online experience. Somewhere along the line he got to know several Russians and tells me that he often takes on editing contracts for Russian writers. Michael is a walking encyclopedia on many subjects but getting details out of him is more than a little difficult. The dark WEB seems to be his playground. He hints about on-going connections to some highly placed folks. But who knows with Michael, the mystery man?

CHAPTER 15

My Grandnephew Nathan's Story

Nathan was born son of David and Tammy. David is my grandnephew.

After graduating high school, he attended college. While in college, he was drafted as a starting pitcher into major league baseball.

He pitched for the Washington Nationals in 2013, Tampa Bay Rays in 2014–2015, Seattle Seahawks in 2016, Kansas City Royals in 2017 up to the end of the 2018 season. We met Nate at his sister Amada's wedding in Arlington, Texas, in early November 2018, where Nate told me that he was a free agent and hopes to sign with another team for the 2019 season. Subsequently, he was signed by the Baltimore Orioles as a starting pitcher.

While a major league pitcher Nate married Jennifer, and in May, the couple had their first child. That will make me a great-great uncle. Am I that old?

Carol and I had had the enjoyment of watching several of his games live and most of his other games on television. The most exciting game I recall, Nathan was pitching for Tampa Bay (an American League team) against an interleague National League team. When Nathan came up to bat, Nathan asked his coach, "What do you want me to do?" The coach said, "Swing away." Nathan hit the ball out of the park for a 1–0 lead. The game ended that way. That has got to be one for the history books.

Good luck, Nate.

Figure 1. Our son, Jonathan, about four years old.

Figure 2. Our son, Jonathan Ned Cole, about six.

Figure 3. Our son, Jonathan Ned Cole, about twenty years old.

*Figure 4. Pittsburg, the way it must have looked
when G. W. Cole arrived in 1820.*

Figure 5. Augustus Cole, my great-grandfather.

Figure 6. Mary Ann Cole, my great-grandmother.

Figure 7. Helen (Henderson) Cole, twenty years old.

Figure 8. Helen, E. P. Cole, and children in 1904.

Figure 9. Harry Murrin as a young man, about 1890.

Figure 10. Harry Murrin, about twenty years old.

Figure 11. My mother, me, and Darlene, about 1946.

Figure 12. Dad on Pennsylvania RR, about 1946.

*Figure 13. My dad and his powerboat, when
he was about seventy years old.*

Figure 14. Dad and two sisters and mother at Bernhoft home, 1950.

Figure 15. Murrin Sister North Park, about 1935.

Figure 16. Mom, Snooky, and Uncle Chuck, about 1938.

Figure 17. Mom and Darlene, 736 McCalmont Street,
Rocky Grove, Pennsylvania, about 1945.

*Figure 18. My sister, Darlene, neighbor, Janice,
and our dog, Brownie, about 1948.*

*Figure 19. Ned Jr., Dave Carter (neighbor),
Darlene, and Cat, about 1951.*

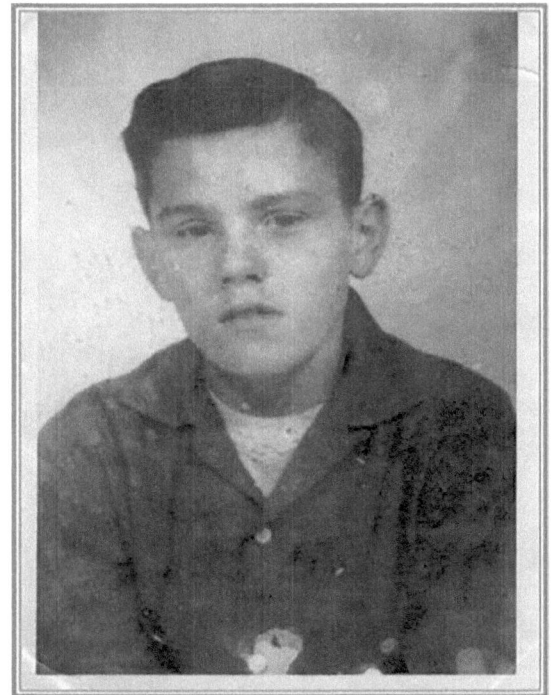

Figure 20. Ned Jr.'s school picture, about 1949.

Figure 21. Ned and Darlene 1960 Florida

Figure 22. Ned, about forty years old.

Figure 23. Ned Jr., Carol, and Carrie, about 1962.

Figure 24. Evelyn (Snooky) Cole, 1955.

Figure 25. Ned Cole Jr., 1958.

*Figure 26. Dad, Ned Jr., and Mom, Slippery
Rock graduation, January 1962.*

Figure 27. Jeff, Jon, Ned, Ben Regina wedding, 1989.

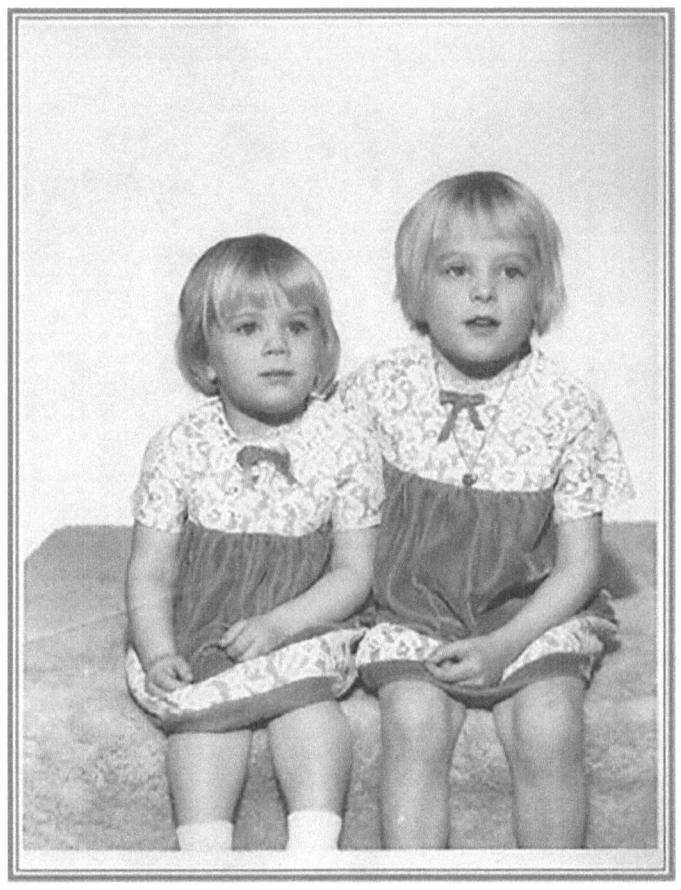

Figure 28. Regina, two and a half, and Carrie, six.

Figure 29. Regina, about five.

Figure 30. Carrie, Bill about 25 and Jeff Reilly just born

Figure 31. Carrie and kids, Jeff and Maddie.

*Figure 32. My uncle, Charles Murrin, and
his wife, Agnes, about 1952.*

Figure 33. Sandy Lake farm grandpa, grandma, my cousins, us kids

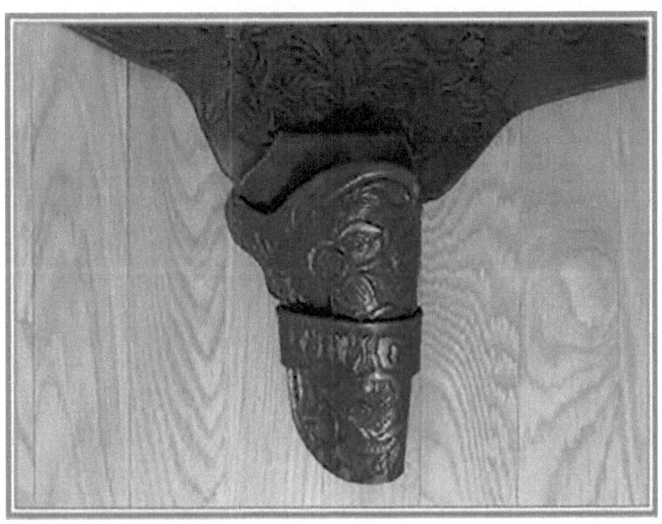

Figure 34. Holster for 38 Colt.

Figure 34. Snooky and Pat's wedding, 1957.

Figure 35. Carol's grandmother and grandfather, John and Mary Hegburg, in their wedding picture, about 1901.

Figure 36. Mary Carol Vensel, third grade, nine years old.

Figure 37. Carol, about fifty-five years old.

Figure 38. Carol and sister Judy, about 2010.

*Figure 39. Carol and Ned's fifty-fifth
wedding anniversary in 2016.*

Figure 40. Carol at Aunt Mary's house, about 1980.

Figure 41. LT Cole, 1963.

Figure 42. Major Ned M. Cole, 1984.

Figure 43. Colonel Ned M. Cole, about 2000.

Figure 44. Presented to Col. Cole upon retirement, 1989, NYANG.

Figure 45. Presented to Major Cole by his
Pittsburgh unit in 1980 by his unit

Figure 46. Carol's sister's Judy's wedding to Ron Gillentine.

Figure 47. My sister, Darlene, 1961.

Figure 48. Carol DAR Function WDC.

Figure 49. Our children, about 1978.

Figure 50. Carol, fifty-three years old.

Figure 51. Carol, 1959.

Figure 52. Cole Family, 1997.

Figure 53. Cole family at River House, January 1998.

Figure 54. Carrie, Jon, Jeff, and Regina, about 1976.

Figure 55. Regina and Scott's wedding.

Figure 56. Ben Cole, about four years old.

Figure 57. Ben, about seven years old.

Figure 58. Stan Mikita Hockey Hall of Fame and Ben, six years old.

Figure 59. Stan Mikita and Ben, about thirty years later.

Figure 60. Coach Ben Chicago Stadium, about 2005.

Figure 61. Anne Bendle, our granddaughter,
about twenty-five years old.

Figure 62. Maddie, my granddaughter, in 2012.

Figure 63. Our raft on the Colorado.

Figure 64. Shooting the Rapids on the Colorado.

Figure 65. Our luxury accommodations on the Colorado.

*Figure 66. Larry DeBoer, Ned Cole, and
Larry Belluchie on the Colorado.*

Figure 67. One of many hikes up Colorado River Cliffs.

Figure 68. First house Carol and Ned owned, Chicopee Falls, Massachusetts.

Figure 69. Our Fitzwatertown Road house, Philly suburb, 1967.

Figure 70. Our house on Tuscawillow, Melbourne, Florida.

Figure 71. My office in China, 1996 and 1997.

Figure 72. One of many fabulous dinners with the Chinese.

Figure 73. Ned dancing with a Chinese lady.

Figure 74. Touring New York with the Chinese.

Figure 75. Touring USA with the Chinese.

Figure 76. Carol and Ned cruising, about 2002.

Figure 77. Hugh Murrin's grave, Murrinsville, Pennsylvania.

Figure 78. Mom and Dad's grave, Rocky Grove, Pennsylvania.

Figure 79. My son Jonathan's grave, West Sunbury, Pennsylvania.

SOURCES

History of Allegheny County 1889

Stolen Fields by Jeanne Boggio

Revolutionary War Bounty Land Grants Awarded by State Governments

Geneology.com

Franklin Herald

Ya All

DAR Patriot Centennial Edition Part I 1990

DAR Patriot Index Centennial Edition Part I A–F

Vital Records of Wells, Maine 1619–1950

New England Marriages Prior to 1700 Vol I

New England Marriages Prior to 1700 Vol II

The Pittsburgh Daily Gazette, January 1, 1875

Official State of Pennsylvania Records filed by Augustus P. Cole

LDS International Genealogy Index, film number 1903706

The Descendants of Robert Henderson of Hendersonville, Pennsylvania, by Oren V. Henderson

Pioneer of Maine and New Hampshire 1623–1660

History of York, Maine, Volume I

History of York, Maine, Volume II

Extensive genealogy facts gathered by my wife, Carol Cole, my daughter, Regina Bendle, Steve Maxi, a cousin removed, and my brother-in-law, Craig Coberly, from countless online records searches and many historical books Carol purchased

Oral history of the Cole family told to Ned M. Cole Jr. by his father, Ned M. Cole, and his grandfather, Everson Cole

The New York Times, December 16, 1921, "Guards His Old Home with Two 6-shooters."
The Coles of Neville Island, Marion and Bob Morse, December 25, 1984
SAR Patriots Index
Google Books page 742 Laws of the General Assembly of the Commonwealth of Pennsylvania
US Census records 1810–1910
Transcript of testimony of Ned M. Cole Sr. and Robert Cole as recorded by Marion Bernhoft in 1985. See appendix

APPENDIX A

Ancestors of Ned M. Cole Jr.

Ned M. Cole Jr.'s Direct Male Lineage Male

Captain Bragdon, county of York, Maine Revolutionary War, First Regiment, company commander. His son, aged eighteen, Eben Bragdon served in his father's company

Samuel Cole born 1710–1720, birthplace unknown, probably Maine

Captain John Cole, Wells, Maine, born April 19, 1740, died Wells, Maine, February 15, 1814, Fourth Company, Revolutionary War

Col. Noah Moulton, First Regiment. Revolutionary War

James Gowen Cole, Wells, Maine, born August 25, 1763, died Allegheny town, Pennsylvania, 1810

George Washington Cole, born 1796, Wells, Maine, died Neville Island, Pennsylvania, December 30, 1874

Augustus P. Cole, born February 5, 1836, Allegheny City, Pennsylvania, died 1889, Neville Island, Pennsylvania, Civil War combat veteran, wounded Everson P. Cole, born October 10, 1887 Neville Island, Pennsylvania, died Fayetteville, New York, September 11, 1966

Ned M. Cole, born March 21, 1911, Neville Island, Pennsylvania, died Sugarcreek Twp. Nursing Home, Pennsylvania, August 15, 1998

Ned M. Cole Jr., born April 1, 1940, USAF/PAANG/NYAng, Colonel (Ret.) Jeffrey James Cole born November 22, 1967 Abington, Pennsylvania, Illinois National Guard Second Lieutenant, honorably discharged, no children Herbert Litt, great-grandfather on my mother's side, born 1857 in Luxembourg (Germany), naturalized about 1895, immigrated to Minnesota in 1890, died in 1925

Ned M. Cole Jr.'s Direct Female Lineage

Abigail (Gowen) Cole, wife of John Cole, born August 23, 1741, died June 26, 1778

Dorcas Woodbridge (Bragdon), wife of George W. Cole, born about 1810 in Sullivan, Hancock, Maine, died April 25, 1881

Ebenezer Bragdon, father of Dorcas

Samuel Bragdon, grandfather of Dorcas

Samuel Bragdon, grandson of Dorcas, born circa 1830, died circa 1905, Civil War veteran 1862–1865, born York County, Maine, died Richmond, New York, married second wife Meritable Hancsom, second wife received pension Joseph Bragdon, great-grandfather of Dorcas

Abigail Cole, first wife of John Cole, died June 11, 177_, died at age thirty-seven

Elizabeth Cole, my great-great-great-great-grandmother, second wife of John Cole

Mary Ann (Dickson) Cole, my great-grandmother, wife of Augustus P. Cole, daughter of James Dickson, born August 18, 1845, Neville Island, Pennsylvania, died April 27, 1933

Robert Henderson, 1741–1810, great-great-grandfather of my grandmother, Helen Elizabeth (Henderson) Cole

John C. Henderson, 1771–1856, great-grandfather of Helen Elizabeth (Henderson) Cole

William Henderson, 1801–1882, grandfather of Helen (Henderson) Cole Harvey Henderson, 1838–1921, father of Helen (Henderson) Cole, Civil War veteran. Tenth Pennsylvania Reserve Infantry. He was twenty-seven years old when he enlisted

Helen Elizabeth (Henderson) Cole, wife of Everson P. Cole, born June 27, 1879, Sandy Lake, Pennsylvania, died June 1975, Sandy Lake, Pennsylvania, at the age of ninety-seven

Andrew Hamilton, 1676–1741, Speaker of the House, Pennsylvania Assembly 1748–1754 1759–1763???

James Hamilton, 1710–1783, son of Andrew, governor of Pennsylvania

Hugh Murrin, great-great-great-grandfather of my mother, born in 1747 in Londonderry, Ireland, died October 27, 1841, married Catherine Shaw, 1780, Revolutionary War New Jersey Regiment, moved to Murrinsville area.

Acquired four hundred acres. His descendants yet own the land as of 2019 Philip Murrin, born 1790, died September 19, 1867 son of Hugh

Joseph Murrin, born 1824, son of Philip

John Chrysostom Murrin, son of Joseph, born April 12, 1821, died?

Joseph Ambrose Murrin, son of John, born May 18, 1885, died about 1949

James Henry Murrin, son of Joseph, my grandfather, born August 18, 1894, died March 1971

Anna Eveline (Murrin) Cole, daughter of James, my mother, wife of Ned M. Cole, born March 27, 1919 Murrinsville, Pennsylvania, died December 15, 1998 Sugarcreek Twp. Nursing Home, Pennsylvania

Anna (Pleats) Litt, great-grandmother on Ned M. Cole Jr.'s mother's side, born in Luxemburg (German) 1870, naturalized citizen about 1895

Lena (Litt) Murrin, wife of Harry Murrin, born in Minnesota, 1891, died in Pittsburgh Pennsylvania, March 19, 1976

Anna Eveline (Murrin) Cole, my mother, daughter of Lena Murrin, born March 27, 1919, Murrinsville, Pennsylvania, died December 15, 1998, Sugarcreek Twp. Nursing Home, Pennsylvania

Ancestors of Ned M Cole Jr. Who Fought or Served in the American Revolutionary War

Captain John Cole, my great-great-great-grandfather, commissioned by John Hancock, served in Fourth Company, Col. Noah Moulton, First Regiment.

Hugh Murrin, my great-great-great-great-grandfather, born in 1747 in Londonderry, Ireland, died October 27, 1841, Pennsylvania Militia

Ebenezer Bragdon Sr., to whom I am directly related, born 1768, York, Maine, Private in Captain Daniel (volunteer) Company, served from July 1779 to September 1779

William Ebenezer Bragdon, to whom I am directly related, enlisted in Captain Sullivan's Company during the Revolutionary War on or about July 28, 1779

William Cole, to whom I am directly related, born November 22, 1740, Maine, died November 26, 1824, Maine, Source NSDAR Patriot Index,

Revolutionary War unit unknown

Arthur Bragdon, to whom I am directly related, private, in Captain Jonathan Nowell Company

Samuel Cole, born 1767, died 1850, Kennebunk, Maine

Ezra Cole, to whom I am directly related, pensioned February 17, 18, died March 3, 1815, corporal, Captain Timothy Company, Colonel Thomas Wigglesworth Regiment. This unit brought back the cannons from Fort Ticonderoga in 1776

Clark Rathbone, my great-great-grandfather, 1778, Captain Joseph Draper Company of Colonel Archibald Kasson under the command of General John Sullivan

William Carroll, my great-great-great-grandfather, captain, born 1741, died 1813, Battle of Cowpens. His son was killed while under William Carroll's command.

Jonathan Rathbone Jr., brother of Clark Rathbone

Thomas Tillinghast, grandfather of Ruth Rathbone. He was too old to fight, so was made civil servant in Rhode Island

Caleb Baldwin, Mendham, New Jersey, died February 19, 181

Benjamin Pitney, born 1720, died 1798, Patriotic Service

These Coles Fought in the Revolutionary War. I May or May Not Be Related to Them.

Thomas Herrick Cole, sergeant, Captain Low Company
William Cole, lieutenant, Captain Pike's First Company
Daniel Bragdon, Company of Captain Turner
Ezekiel Bragdon, private, of J Lane
Ezra Cole, private, Nathaniel Cousens Company
John Bragdon, private, Company of Captain S. Derby Lieutenant Henry Cole 2nd
Francis Cole, private, Captain Sabin Man Company
Francis Cole, corporal, Captain Nathaniel Heath Company
Gail Cole, private, Captain Stephen Bedlam Artillery Company
Gersham Cole, private, Captain John Bridgham Company
Georoe Cole, private, Elijah Crooker Company
Hezekiah Cole, private, Lieutenant Noah Dickenson Company
Hezekiah Cole, private, Captain Nathaniel Shaw Company
Hezekiah Cole, private, Captain Jeremiah Miller Company
Hezekiah Cole, private, Captain Peleg Peck Company
Isaac Cole, seaman, ship commanded by Captain Simeon Samson

Ancestors of Ned M Cole Jr., Who Fought in the American Civil War

Ivory S. Cole, my great-great uncle, enlisted private, April 4, 1865, Company C, 198th Infantry, Regiment Ohio, Honorably discharged April 8,1865, Camp Bradford, Baltimore, Maryland, his father was Rufus Cole of Pennsylvania Augustus P. Cole, Company K 123rd Infantry Regiment, Colonel Clark commanding, Pennsylvania, from August 9,1862 to May 13,1863. Fought at Fredericksburg, Antietam, South Mountain, and Chancellorsville. Wounded at battle of Fredericksburg.

Harvey Heath Henderson, enlisted as a private in Company G, 39 Regiment Pennsylvania (10 Reserve), Union Army at Mercer, July 8, 1861. Honorably discharged 1865 Engaged in many battles with eastern Union armies

Captain Horace S. Cole

Lemuel N. Cole

Henry M. Cole

Nathan C. Cole

APPPENDIX B

- Did you think of yourseves as rich kids ?
N- No, but I did appreciate the beauty. I never considered myself
   rich. No, I was never rich and never will be.
- Were there people on the island who seemed to be better off
   than you folks ?
N- No, I don't think there was.
- How about sickness ? Can you remember your grandmother's last
   sickness ?
N- My grandmother was brought up the the farm at Sandy Lake after
   the trouble on the island. Both my grandmother and my father
   had stayed down trying to more or less guard the place, more
   look after it after Dad had sent the rest of us to Sandy Lake.
   I think this kind of affected her some because she really loved
   it when she lived down there. She came up -- I think she was
   88 when she died. My mother looked after her but she could
   still see the boats going down the river. That's how her mind
   was affected some for the trouble she went through. There was
   no river and no boats because this was out in the country. We
   still were able to live well. ---- Lay in bed and she'd say
   " Oh Ned, there goes the Homer Smith! " or "Oh Ned, don't you
   see the Aroclipa going down ?" They were paddle wheelers push-
   ing barges and she imagined----. Then I'd kinda go along with
   her and she'd be satisfied.
- Did she seem to be a very loving person ?
N- No, grandma was not a mean person but she wasn't a real out-
   going person. She'd hold herself a little too stiff and reserved. She was very reserved.
- Did she seem to have a good relationship with your grandfather ?
N- I think they did from what I heard. Grandma, like I said was
   always a proud woman. After we'd moved up to Sandy Lake she
   started getting hairs on her chin and grandma would give me a
   penny a hair for pulling those hairs out.
- You must have made a lot of money ?
N- Oh no ! But grandma would always give me money on the side.
- How was the relationship between your Mom and grandmother Cole ?
N- Not too good though I never heard them squabble-- but even as
   a child I could feel a little something there.
- They both lived in the same house ?
N- They lived in the same house but it was divided. They each
   had their own side of the house and each kept their side quite
   well. But we children could go over to Grandma Cole's side any
   time we wanted and she was always real good to me.
- Down on Neville Island, I understand some real problems developed in relation to the sale of the property. How old were you
   then ?
N- It started when I was 5 years old and finally my first recollection
   was during the war-- First world war. --- Several men came and
   notified my father that he had to vacate and my father wasn't
   about to lose the place but the government was condemning the
   place to put up a munitions plant. Then the next thing-- we had
   what was called "the pickle house" where they boiled the horse
   radish and bunched the asparagus which my Dad sold wholesale.
   Anyhow, for some unknown reason, that was set on fire and it was

187

N- Enough to buy a farm and build a house.
 - Tell us about Sandy Lake.
N- Dad bought this farm and was going to remodel the house. I
   recall one day Dad got disgusted and he said "Tear it down".
   "Just save the kitchen". So they tore the whole thing down and
   started from scratch. Well, when the neighbors around there saw
   the house my Dad was building they said,"Boy, that guy's rich !"
   --- and they thought he was, which he wasn't but he got along
   alright. Anyhow, we were the first folks to have electricity,
   running water in the house, a bathroom in the house and that
   was something in those days that very few people had. We
   bought a new car and a new truck so we just did our act. It
   was a nice farm though.   Dad would pick out things to raise
   that had a lot of work to them like 7 acres of asparagus, a lot
   of cabbage and anywhere from 12 to 20 acres of potatoes and they
   all had to be hoed at that time.
 - Back to Neville island days. How did your Mom and Dad meet ?
N- They met in Bellevue at an aunts. It so turned out that this
   aunt and uncle (the uncle) was related to my Dad and the aunt
   to my Mom. It was across from the island.
 - How'd they get along ?
N- They got along the same the same as normal folks, Mother never
   did like the island--- her heart was always around Titusville
   and Sandy Lake. She was a Henderson and was born in Titusville
   and was at Hendersonville named after her relatives. My mother
   was always trying to pull back towards Sandy Lake. In the long
   run, mother was glad to leave the island while my father and
   grandmother weren't. That's where their roots were.
 - Was your Dad a good guy ? Was he good looking ?
N- Oh, I don't know. I don't think you know whether your folks are
   good looking or not. On the farm, Dad was a very hard worker. One
   thing about my father, if hay lay in the field come Sunday, it
   lay there until Monday. But I don't think he ever lost by it.
   That was one day that we didn't go out into the fields to work.
   We did our chores and what work we had to do. We ate well on Sun-
   days as far as that goes but that's one thing about my dad, he
   never went out to the hay field or anything though some of the
   other farmers under some circumstances did so.
 - Is it true he did a lot of travelling ?
N- Yes, Dad did quite a lot while he was young and up until he was
   married. He was fortunate enough and was over in Europe and he
   took one trip to Spain that I heard quite a lot about just before
   he was married and then he worked in Colorado. He liked to work
   around the mines. He kept trying and trying but Dad never quite
   made it at mining. But he did work hard at whatever he did, I'll
   say that for my father. He provided well for us during the depression. There wasn't as much money at that time because he had
   lost heavily in the stock market. There was never a time that we
   weren't well filled and had good clothes to wear.
 - Was he a quiet type person ?
N- Well-------I do remember dad was mad about something, I don't
   know what it was over but he was down at the barn. There was one
   horse that would playfully take a hold of him. Jim, the horse,
   took a hold of Dad's arm and got a little bit of skin when he did
   it. Dad turned around and swore at him and then actually kicked

liked the farm. Uncle Jim wound up as an engineer on the
Pennsylvania and Lake Erie railroad.
- Do you think that your father was more favored by his mother ?
N- I always felt that my father was more favored by his mother --
perhaps it was because my Dad stayed there. Because that is
where my grandmother's and my father's hearts were--- right
on the truck garden on the far m.
- What do you remember about the truck garden ? What did they
raise ? How did a day go ?
N- It was relly nice to get up in the morning and look across when
the produce was coming on because they raised asparagus and horse
radish to grind and sell and they raised tomatoes and rhubarb
but my father always kepthis fields so clean. He hired four who
stayed all the time in the rooms he had inour buildings and then
he hired extra hands during the busy season. I can still picture them out there with their hoes. There may have been up
to nine fellows in a row hoeing across the fields. Dad, I'd say
was a rich truck gardener. At that time Dad would get up at 4
o'clock in the morning, load up his wagon, and he kept beautiful
horses, with harnesses all shined up and the brass and leather
all oiled. I can still see this large green sided high wagon and
that's what Dad would tale his produce in up to the market in
town. (Pittsburgh). Most of it would be sold wholesale and then
he would go to retail off the wagon up in the bottoms of McKee's
rocks and around the Pittsburgh area. Then later on, when I got
to be12-14, he got a Studebaker truck and to this day that
truck reminds me of a nail crate on the front end and an orange
crate on the back end. The next year he bought a Republic truck.
That had solid rubber wheels and was chain driven.
- Was there a bridge from the island ?
N- Oh yes, I don't know when they were built. There was one at the
head of the island we called "The Park Bridge", then at the other
end was the Coraopolis bridge. Those were across the back river.
There was no bridge across the front river. We always went the
back way to get to the mainland.
- Were there trolley cars ?
N- Yes, the trolley cars came from Pittsburg to the head of the
island and down the middle of the island at that time and then
across the Coraopolis bridge at the lower end to Coraopolis and
that's where they turned around and ran back up. We had good
trolley service then. The one year I went to school, I rode the
street car.
- your folks owned about 5 and one half acres ?
N- Yes, then my Dad rented some ground too. Back in the bottoms
there was some real good ground.
To show you what my Dad was like--- when we moved to Sandy Lake,
he set up a chicken farm along with the other farming. I can't
say how many hens he had--- perhaps a thousand. He got top prices
in Pittsburgh for the eggs-- he sold them by the case. Every egg
was candled--- that was to look through to see if there was any
spot on them and every egg was stamped with the date. He got
top prices from McCanns and they took all the eggs he could pro- .

duce. Finally in the Fall, the coop burned -- we never knew
what happened.
- He seemed to have had quite a bit of bad luck.
N- Dad had bad luck. He was a man who always tried to make it good
and we always had enough. He always gave us what he had.
- Back on Neville, How did your mother fit into the gardening and
the family business ?
N- Mother didn't work out in the fields, of course, but we did
feed quite a few hired hands. I can remember a long table in
our kitchen. Mother had a lady helper. Her name was Mrs. Morgan.
And she generally had someone to help with the cleaning but it was
a lot of work for my mother. We had at least 4 regular hired
hands. Other part time hands we called "foreigners" would eat
out in the entry--- there was a table out there.
- How come you didn't stay in farming ?
N- Well, I really liked the food that was produced on the farm but
I didn't like the hoeing used to produce it. I could stand it
just so long and then I would take off for a while but eventually
I came back. My heart just wasn't in it. At one time I was interested in starting a beef and hog farm because we had a good com-
bination but everybody couldn't fight C.I.I.. So I figured the
best thing to do was to work for the railroad. I ended up in train
service whereas Uncle Jim was in engine service. I'm really glad
I did--- I had a good life on the railroad and a good home life.
- Do you feel there was warmth between your Mom and Dad ?
N- Yes, there was warmth there, but at times I couldn't understand
everything. My Dad really left my mother, My mother really loved
my Dad but I don't think she really loved my Dad as much as he
loved her. Don't misunderstand me, my mother was a very good
woman and I don't think she ever did anything she thought was
wrong. If she did anything that was wrong, I'm sure she didn't
realize it. I had a very good mother and my dad was always good
to me. I have happy memories of my father sitting and reading to
me and talking to me. I'd say they had an average marriage relationship. There was kindness in our home.

-------The interview continues with Bob Cole in Sandy Lake
the next day. --------------------

- How old were you when you left Neville Island ?
B- About 17
- Tell us about the eviction.
B- Yes, I was there. The police backed up about 4 steps, mounted
police came to our back door, rapped on it, and handed the eviction papers. Dad says" I'm not taken that and I'll give you this".
He pulled out two guns. So Lawrence, he was the chief, left --
and said "Boys, you take care of it". They never did. Then things
went from bad to worse.
- Did you leave soon after that ?
B- Oh No, it must have been at least three or four months. I toted
a rifle for about a year, lost a year at school, didn't go anywhere. Didn't do us any good, two attorneys that we had, court
costs, nearly everything was gone before we left.
- Who were your attorneys ?
B- Replogle was one from Pittsburgh and there was one from California. They took one third plus and took the plus first.
- Tell us about your early boyhood.
B- Grandma was a large woman. She wasn't fat but she was big. She
wore black silk most of the time-- occasionally a white shirt-

190

waist --- shoe topper skirts. You could hear grandma coming
clear around the corner of the house with her silks swishing. She
was friendly and warm, a whole lot like my mother. She was law.
She ran the show and she was asked for advice by a great many
people on the island.
- Did you feel better off than most of the folks on the island ?
B- Lot of excitement --- more than they had by far. Yeah, but we
had good food. Dad was a good provider always.
- Did you go to market with him ?
B- Only to the stand in Pittsburgh -- up in Smallwood Street.
- How did you go ?
B- Streetcar. The vegetables went by wagon and later by truck. We
had special wagons -- had a 5 inch tire (steel) -- special make.
We had big Clysdale horses-- the driver took care of it and sometimes - most of the time when they'd get up on the wagon, they'd
snap themselves on-- that is 2 straps so they couldn't fall off
from the seat which was up over the wagon. The horses were educated so when street cars would come along in back and gong the
bell a half dozed times, the horses would cross off to the side
where there was room. We had special racks for the tomatoes and
they were put on shelves and would go between cross boards and
you could pile them closer that way. We'd have as high as seven
tiers of tomatoes. Then cabbage and sweet corn wecould just pile
on top of each other. Wagons came up 3 feet then have a floor
board and then 2 feet more and then we'd pile a tier on top of
that. We'd take that in early in the morning so it would be there
before the stores would open up. Sometimes one buyer would
purchase for 5 or 6 stores. So we had to be   there before or
we'd just be out of luck. We were the wholesaler. There were
two sets of them. One would be Smallman street where we unloaded
it and then some of the smaller bars they would come into them.
Then someone like H.J. Heinz would take as high as 2 or 3 full
loads. There would be as many as 90 bushels of corn on and they
would go 8 tiers high. One wagon we weren't allowed to use.
They cut us off on account of safety. They said that when it
would be raining one of the men might get electrocuted. Now this
is far fetched. Sometimes the rain would run down the trolley
from the hill and there'd be a steady stream of water and maybe-
just maybe, they'd get grounded on the street car tracks. The
tires on the wagon were steel. So we had to abandon that wagon.
- Did you have an automobile in those days ?
B- We had the fourth truck that was in Allegheny county, Dad or John
Eckert usually drove the truck in . John used to be our good man
(foreman). He finally went beserck. He was going to kill uncle
Finley -- gonna shoot him. Dad stopped him. That was some fight,
I'm telling you, when a person goes crazy in a time of fire or
something like that you're at least twice as strong as you
ordinarily are. Dad almost didn't make it. John was going to
shoot him. Just the mercies of God, that's all.
- You mentioned earlier that your mother had an operation.
B- I don't know the reason for the operation over in Sewickley, but
she was in for hours. There were five doctors and back about ten
years ago the last one died. After mother was brought home we
didn't think she'd live. They had her on the meat cart. They
thought she was dead. Miss Lavis, our family nurse -----. The
Sewickley hospital, the old one, the corridors used to be along
side--- and they had cross aleey ways and mother was on the cart
which was against the wall and they had a black schrobe (sheet)

on her waiting for the meat grinder to come. One of the nurses went by and she thought she saw the blanket move and she turned around and it fell to the floor. Well, she screamed and fainted. That was before they embalmed. ---- She was chief cook and bottle washer, took care of the kids. We had hired help for the pickle house. We grew corn and tomatoes and at one time, egg plants pattipans (never looked for regular squash though). Asparagus was our major. Five and one half acres on the island. We double planted--- two rows instead of one row which was equivalent to 11 acres. Neville island asparagus was very well liked. The soil on the island was the tops in vegatable growing ground. The top soil was anywhere from 1 and a half feet deep to 4 feet deep.

- Do you remember industry starting at the end of the island while you were still farming ?
B- Oh yes. That had been going on for years. When you make the right hand turngoing East towards Pittsburgh from Coraopolis back tothe back river, this along the West side toward that river, that was the Neville Oil refineries.
- What were the names of some of the boats that ent down the river ?
B- "Iron City" was a commercial boat, "P.M. Piffle", "Sunshine" was the only side wheeler and the "Homer" was a stern wheeler. And they brought another one in there that didn't have any name. It was a boot leg boat so they said and it didn't have a license.
- Do you remember the dam going in ?
B- Oh yes! There was perminent concrete in after they poured the coffer dam. It was aboult a half mile from our house. Dad paid $10,000 for that one acre there so they would have to trespass.
- Tell us about the troubled times in 1919.
B- They were cutting a path along the river and they came up with steam shovels right up to our front porch. They went down to Uncle (Tom ?) Hamilton's that was about ½ mile below our place and that's where they ended it. What they did, they knew was wrong, but they were just after their ten million dollars. It was to lay the foundations for the power house, it was a 90 feet drop. Ginnys and Mexicans were on this long ladder and the ladder broke and covered a lot of them up.
- Was your house the only one left at that time ?
B- Yes we were holding the fort. On Dickson Ave. in Avalon, Uncle Gerny built 6 houses. The Dicksons scattered around. Uncle Finley went to Crafts, Uncle Wils went to Coraopolis and Uncle John-- I think was dead.
- When you moved to Sandy Lake how did it work ?
B- Corrine was with us for quite a while then they sent her up to Sandy Lake and went one year, Dad stayed on the island and was foreman on the Ensworth dam for about 2 years.
- Picture being shown of a machine.
B- This machine is what they used to drill test holes. They drilled about 90 or 100 of them. They went down about 80 ft. Well this was the last day that this fella freely used this equipment. Used to be an old bath tub which sat over here and they had about 5 acres of 'pattipans" (squash) and one side of the field was surplus and they were half rotten. We took and piled dozens of them

in this tub of water and it gummed everything up. He was here
about a week. When we'd go down past it, the road was abot 50
feet away, they were saying "Oh I wish we knew who did that!".
Well, they knew--- all those fellows around there were on our
side, definitely. ------ What we used to do ------ We'd have
been put in jail if it had been anyplace else. They were 100%
for us. We two kids had lots of fun !
- Picture of two kids with strings of fish.
B- That's me and that's Jack Myers. Those sacks-- Purina food
sacks. We had been just one hour fishing. Nellie Platt was the
best school teacher that ever could be, ordinarily we had a class
the last period in 7th grade and Nellie knew our clothes came
from fish and she had changed classes around for that period.
When buckwheat season was in, that's when fish would travel in
the Fall. Nellie would change from class to study and then she'd
let him go (Jack M.), he didn't do any studying-- she'd push
him through high school. He was one of our steady helpers. One
would get at one end of the bank and the other right down below
where our disposal plant is now -- in Sandy Lake-- when it was
buckwheat time then they would stop the flow-- the dam would
fill the mill race, there would be no water running because it
was feeding the mill race. The creek would go down to practically
nothing. Well the fish knew that the water was getting shallow
and they just go to this hole -- and that went on for two years
and the other fellows were not wise to it. Nothing unusual to
have a full string of fish. We had our whole set of customers
in Sandy Lake. We sold two fish for a quarter. We did very well.
This was while we were living with Grandma Henderson. ----- We
swung the first pick and ax to put in the splinter works in
Sandy Lake. ("Splinter works" is where pallets are made.) I'd
been the first one to work in 3 plants in Sandy Lake. No more
than you'd get laid off one when something else would come up.
Where the splinter works is now, I caught a mink. I caught an
Otter where there used to be an overflow to the mill race. It's
almost all gone now.
- Picture of dump trucks
B- The dump carts in the picture were the ones used to make that
cut in front of the house on the island. There were 5 of them
and they were cut down to three. When they quit their work at
night there would be " fire up". The fellas would just chop the
old thing and pull the throttles back and set the brakes and then
just jump off and go home. We would jump on, take the blocks out
and pull the throttle back and they'd go over to the end and
fall down into the hole. That would slow them up another day or
two. --- We'd pull her back and jump off and away she'd go.
- Picture
B- This picture shows one of the holes that bored in underneath and
around two water mains that went from the upper end of the island
down where the steel companies had their thousand Mexicans that
were doing the work on the island. Right here at the bottom of
the clock, we'd go down there and shut the water off.
- Did your mother know you were doing these things ?
B- She didn't know we were doing a thing. She wouldn't have stopped
us-- she was just as provoked. The steam engine had a chain on
it so we couldn't do the same thing with it. We did lock the wheel
on it for four days. Dad defied them. He stood right there with

N- See-- Dad bought a plantation down in Virginia but it was a
swindle. He'd already bought mules, he'd bought hogs and was
going to move down there. He evev sent a box car load furniture.
He was gonna send 'em down there and John E. Walker came up to
our place. I remember him and he turned out to be a swindler -
---. Mom was happy, we moved to Sandy Lake. ---- So, I guess
the old folks did have a little money. ---- Well, I think I
know where the balance went---- Nothing against Dad-- the final
line--- lost it all.
B- Just one more turnover !
N- Just one more tuenover !
B- I"ll divide it between you and mother !
He had a private phone between the island, No, between Sandy
Lake and Pittsburgh.
N- But Dad went down and stayed down there and he --- remember,
he was going down for one last turnover 'cause Dad knew it was
coming, But he took that one last gamble and he lost it -- all
on the margin. Make it big and lose it big.
- He must have been doing well at that time.
B- He was, but what good did it do us ?
N- I had a lot of fun going up to Stoneborough picking out a new
car 'cause Dad had told me he'd get it for me when he came back.
He lost it.
- How did he act when he came home ?
N- Oh -- couldn't leave him alone.
- 'Fraid he might shoot himself ?
N- Yup--- stayed right with him.
B- He was berserk, mercies of Gad, that's all--- that and prayer.
N- Dad realized that he didn't only do it with his money but he lost
money that should have gone to other people. I don't hold it agin
Dad, if Dad had of made it, we would have had it. --- We never
had a day hungry if you stayed home which I always didn't ---
always had good clothes.
- Those are the fortunes of war.
N- many jumped out of windows.
B- One time when I was taking produce down to Pittsburgh-- maybe
you never heard of "High Level Bridge", I saw a man jump off
and all he had left on when he hit the cobblestones was just
shoes.
- Those were tough days.

194

APPENDIX C

ADDITIONAL REVOLUTIONARY WAR ANCESTOR DOCUMENTATION FOUND BY REGINA BENDLE

DAR Ancestor #

COLE, JOHN
Ancestor #: A024172
Service: MASSACHUSETTS   Rank(s): CAPTAIN
Birth: 4-19-1740   WELLS YORK CO ME DIST MASSACHUSETTS
Death: 2-15-1814   WELLS YORK CO ME DIST MASSACHUSETTS
Service Source: COPY OF ORIGINAL COMMISSION, IN DOCUMENTATION WITH DAR #609232
Service Description: **1)** COL NOAH MOULTON, MILITIA
    RESIDENCE
    1) **City:** WELLS - **County:** YORK CO - **District:** ME DIST - **State:** MASSACHUSETTS
    SPOUSE
    1) ABIGAIL GOWEN
    2) ELIZABETH EATON

BRAGDON, EBENEZER
Ancestor #: A013624
Service: MASSACHUSETTS   Rank(s): PRIVATE
Birth: CIRCA 1745
Death: ANTE 5-25-1807   SULLIVAN HANCOCK CO MAINE
Service Source: MA SOLS & SAILS, VOL 2, P 427
Service Description: **1)** CAPT. DANIEL SULLIVAN
    RESIDENCE
    1) **City:** SULLIVAN - **County:** LINCOLN CO - **District:** MAINE DIST - **State:** MASSACHUSETTS
    SPOUSE
    1) JANE WILLSON

CARROLL, WILLIAM
Ancestor #: A019796
Service: PENNSYLVANIA   Rank(s): PRIVATE
Birth: 1745   IRELAND
Death: ANTE 5-20-1848   WOLF CREEK TWP MERCER CO PENNSYLVANIA
Service Source: PA ARCH, 5TH SER, VOL 5, PP 60-61, 422-423
Service Description: **1)** CAPT THOMAS ASKEY, COL JAMES DUNLAP
2) CUMBERLAND MILITIA
    RESIDENCE
    1) **County:** CUMBERLAND CO - **State:** PENNSYLVANIA
    SPOUSE
    1. JOANNA WAKEFIELD